From San Servolo to Amalfi

从“疯人岛”到阿玛尔菲

吕澎

从"疯人岛"到阿玛尔菲

—— "给马可波罗的礼物"的散记

Lü Peng

From San Servolo to Amalfi

Notes of a Chinese Curator in Venice

CHARTA

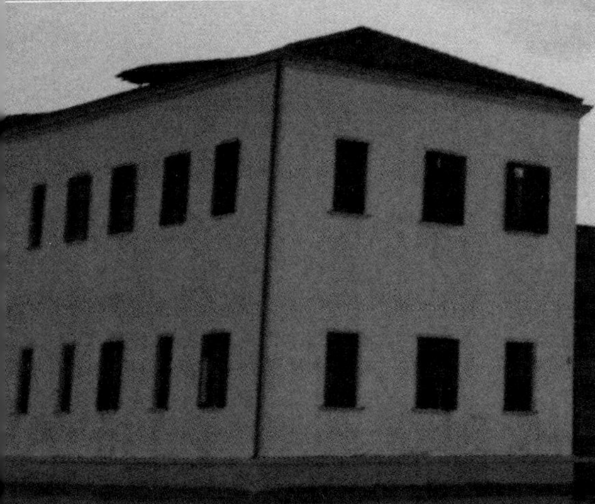
TOBUY IS TOCREATE

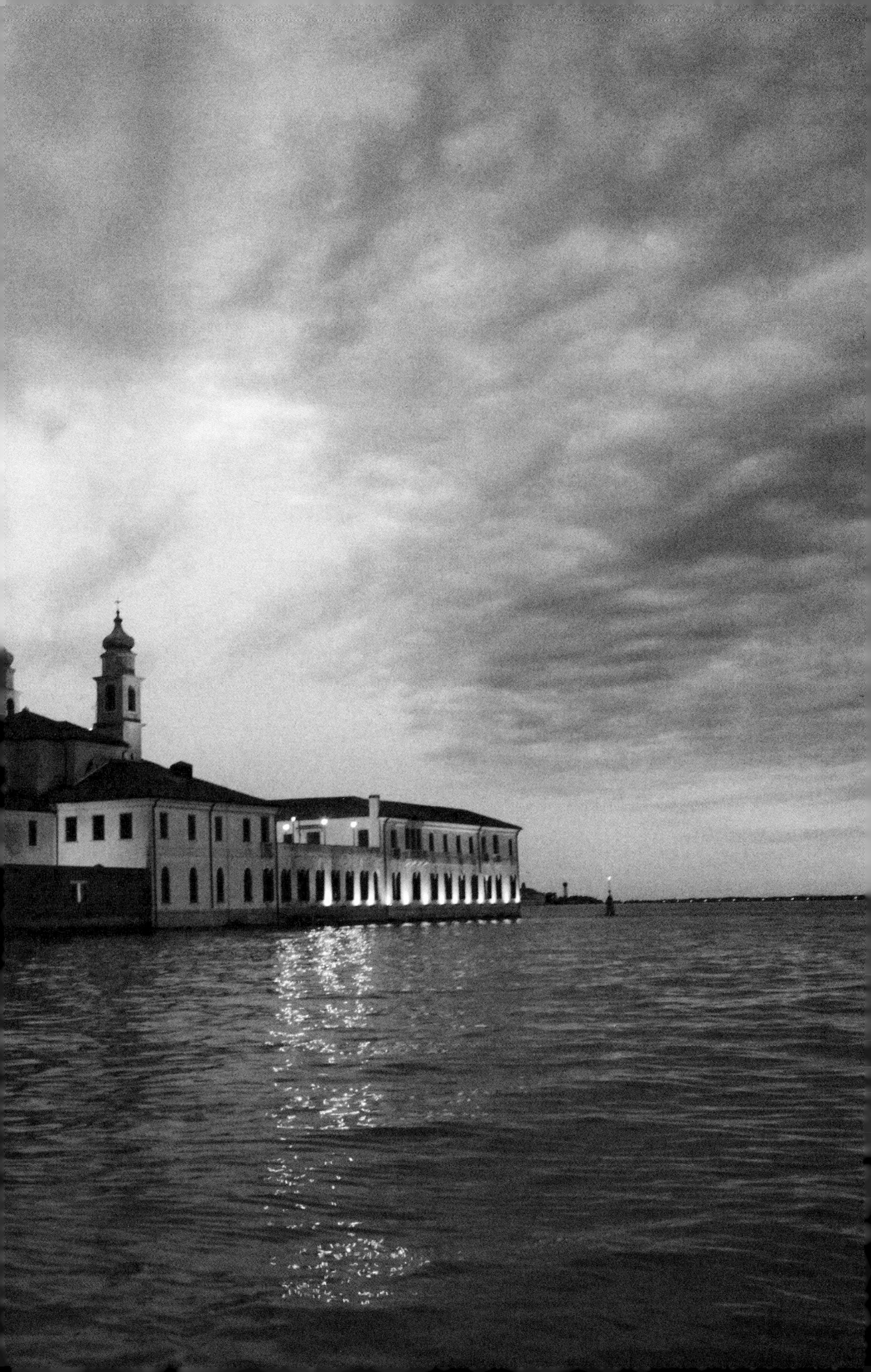

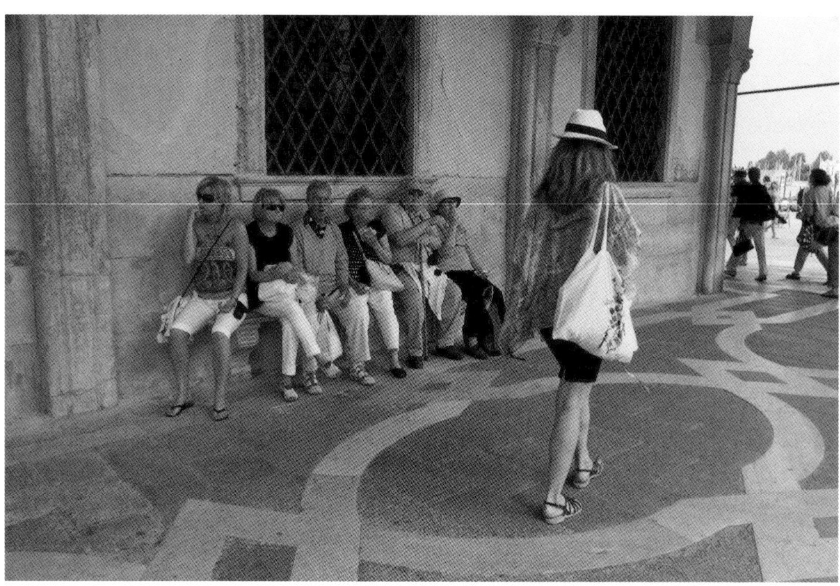

In late February while preparing for the exhibition "A Gift to Marco Polo," I leafed through *The Treasures of Venice* (White Star Publishers), purchased at a Venice bookstore, and learned that in the ninth century the island of San Servolo had once been home to a Benedictine monastery. From the twelfth century until 1715 a group of nuns had been in charge and had built a hospital for soldiers. From 1734 to 1749 a church was constructed there. Later some buildings were converted for use as an insane asylum, which was not closed until 1978. It is easy to imagine this lone island being used for an insane asylum: it is charmingly scenic,

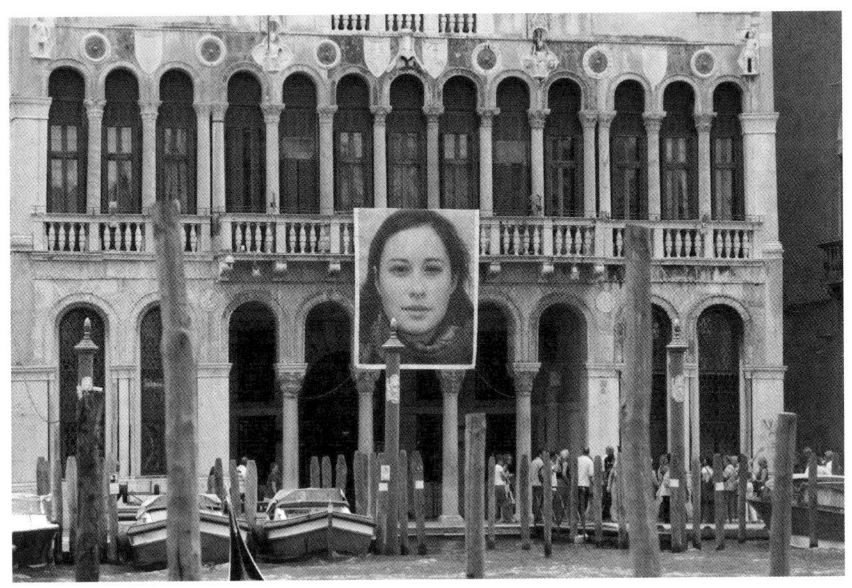

2月底，我因为筹备展览，从在威尼斯的书店里买到的 *The Treasures Of Venice* (White Star Publishers) 中得知，在9世纪，San Servolo 是本笃会教士居住的地方，从12世纪至1715年，主要由修女操持，她们在这里为士兵修建了一所医院。1734到1749年，这里修建了教堂。以后，部分建筑被转而作为精神病院，直到1978年才关闭。把这个孤独的小岛用作精神病院是可以想象的，她美丽、孤独，却与城市没有过分遥远的距离，方便，适合于家人的关怀与探望——我想是这样。我并不知道 San Servolo 详细的历史，我也没有非常的探究心去了解她的过去，从圣马可广场坐船去 San Servolo，只需要十分钟左右的时间。灿烂的阳光下，我们能够非

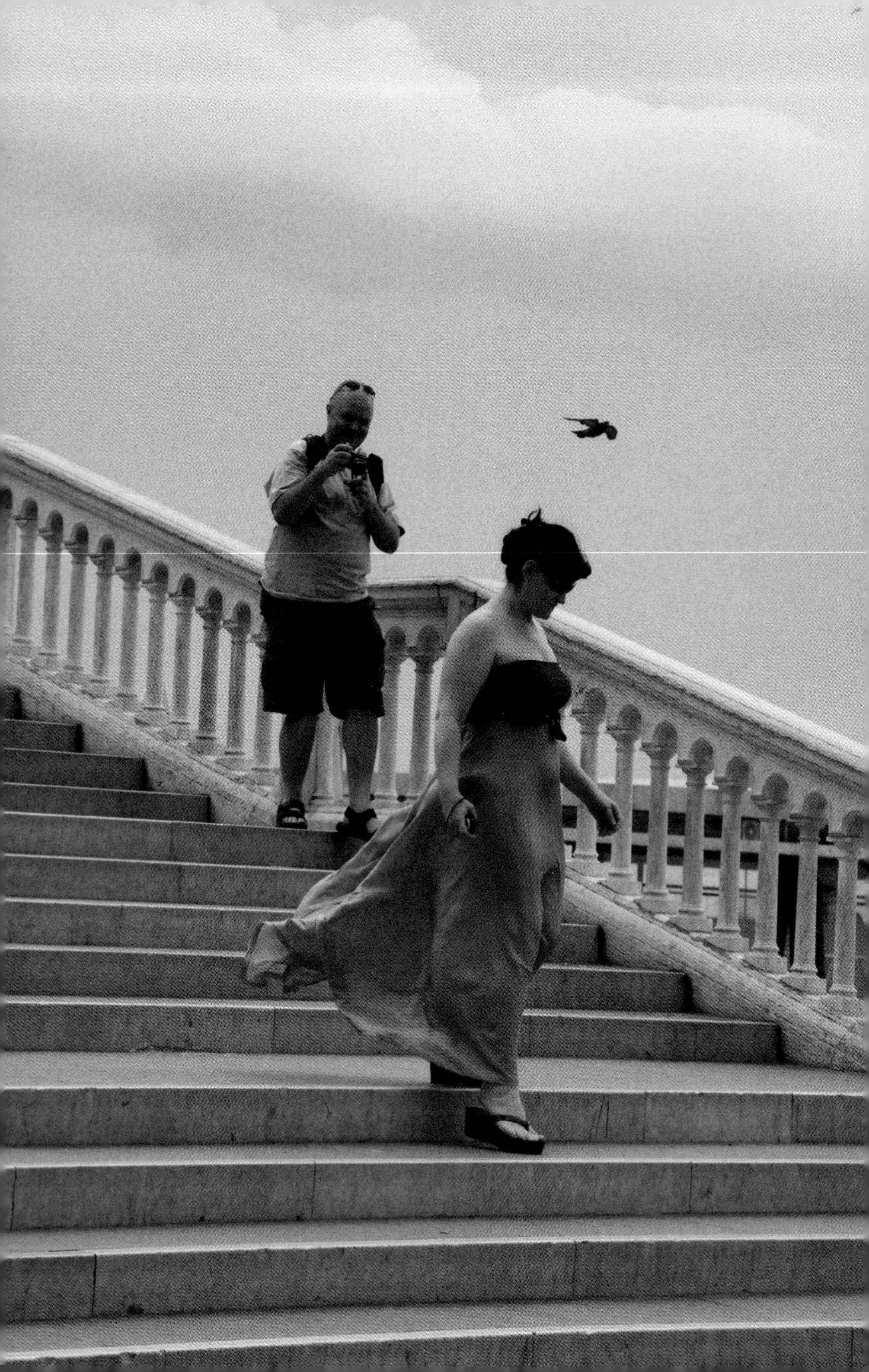

常清晰地看到她。不过，在绵绵的雨天，透过迷蒙的空气，只能依稀看到她的模样。在第一次登上 San Servolo 的时候，我拍了几张有水滴痕迹的照片，不能否认的是，我喜欢 San Servolo 她的建筑，教堂与花园，不是别的原因，仅仅是因为她的相貌告诉我了时间及其含义。的确，与威尼斯其他地方相比，San Servolo 没有特别的不同，甚至也没有特别的建筑，不过是曾经有修士、士兵和精神病人居住和使用过的地方，而今天，她是威尼斯国际大学 (Venezia International University) 的校园。如果不是要举办"给马可波罗的礼物"这个展览，也许再多的威尼斯之行，我也很可能不会登上这个空间非常有限的小岛，而事实上，我已经不少次数登上了她，游历了她，我透过她的视线，观看了岛外的风景，眺望了远处本岛上的建筑与人群，目送了不同形状与速度的船只，领略了大雨将致的乌云以及黄昏中的彩霞。我承认，对于那些长期居住在垃圾般的城市环境中的人来说，的确可以用"美丽"这类我们已经长期不使用的词汇去形容 San Servolo，并且丝毫不会让人感觉到牵强、尴尬与做作。

isolated, yet not too remote from the city. That must have made it convenient for family visits. I do not know the detailed history of San Servolo, and I feel no pressing urge to explore her past. A boat from Piazza San Marco to San Servolo takes only ten minutes. In bright sunlight we can see the island with crystal clarity, but in drizzling rain she looms as a vague shape. The first time I stepped ashore and took a few photographs, my lens was flecked with water beads. My fondness for San Servolo—for her architecture, her church and gardens—is undeniable, simply because her countenance carries a message of time. Admittedly, there is no special difference between San Servolo and Venice, and the little island's architecture is not really remarkable. She was simply a place utilized and dwelled upon by nuns, soldiers, and mental patients. As for now, she is the campus of Venice International University (V.I.U.). Had it not been for the "Gift to Marco Polo" exhibition, I might never have set foot on the confines of this little island, no matter how many trips to Venice I were to take. But in fact I have set foot there numerous times and have seen all her sights. I have borrowed her vantage point to view the cityscape; I have gazed on buildings and crowds on the main island; my eyes have followed boats of various shapes and sizes; I have enjoyed watching masses of dark clouds and rosy tinted clouds at sunset. Long-term urban dwellers might think of words such as "lovely" to describe San Servolo, and such a description would not seem strained or contrived.

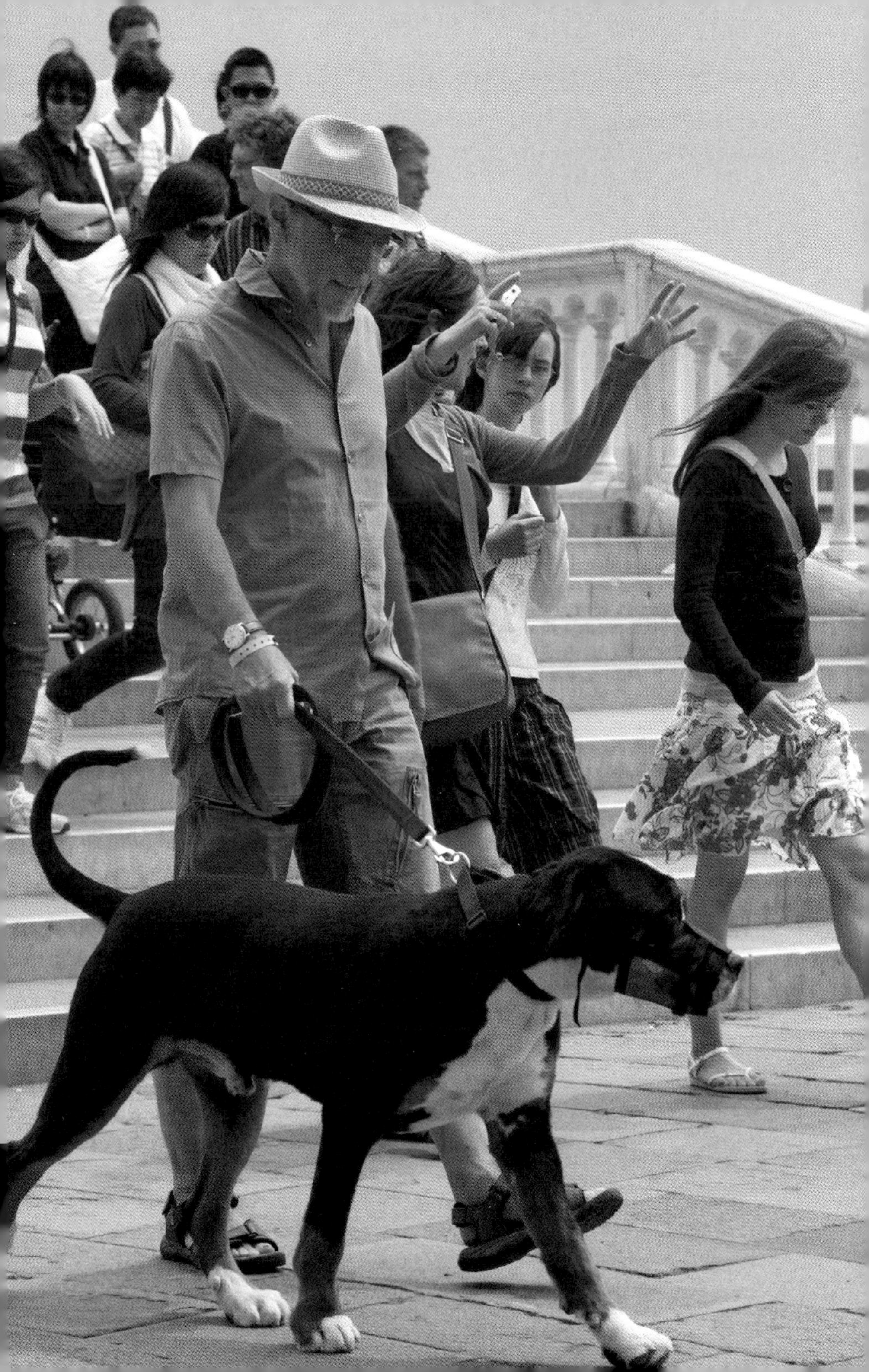

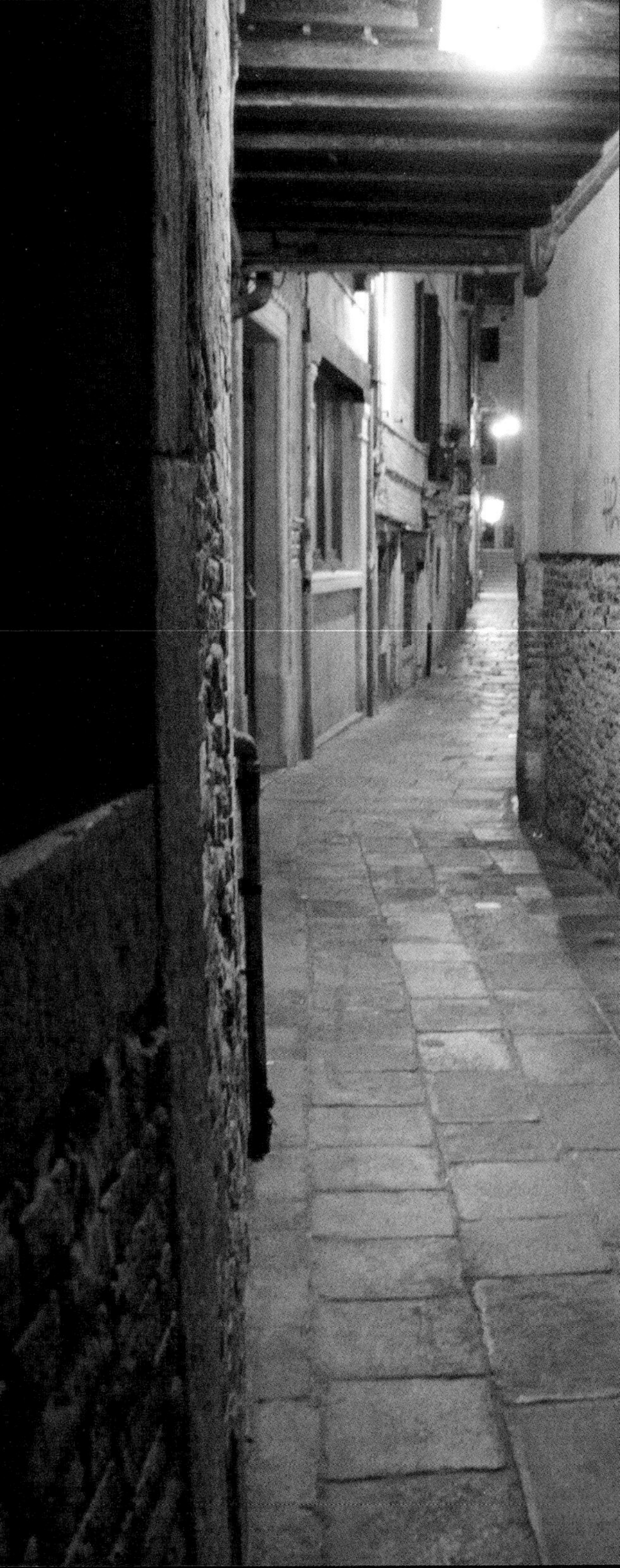

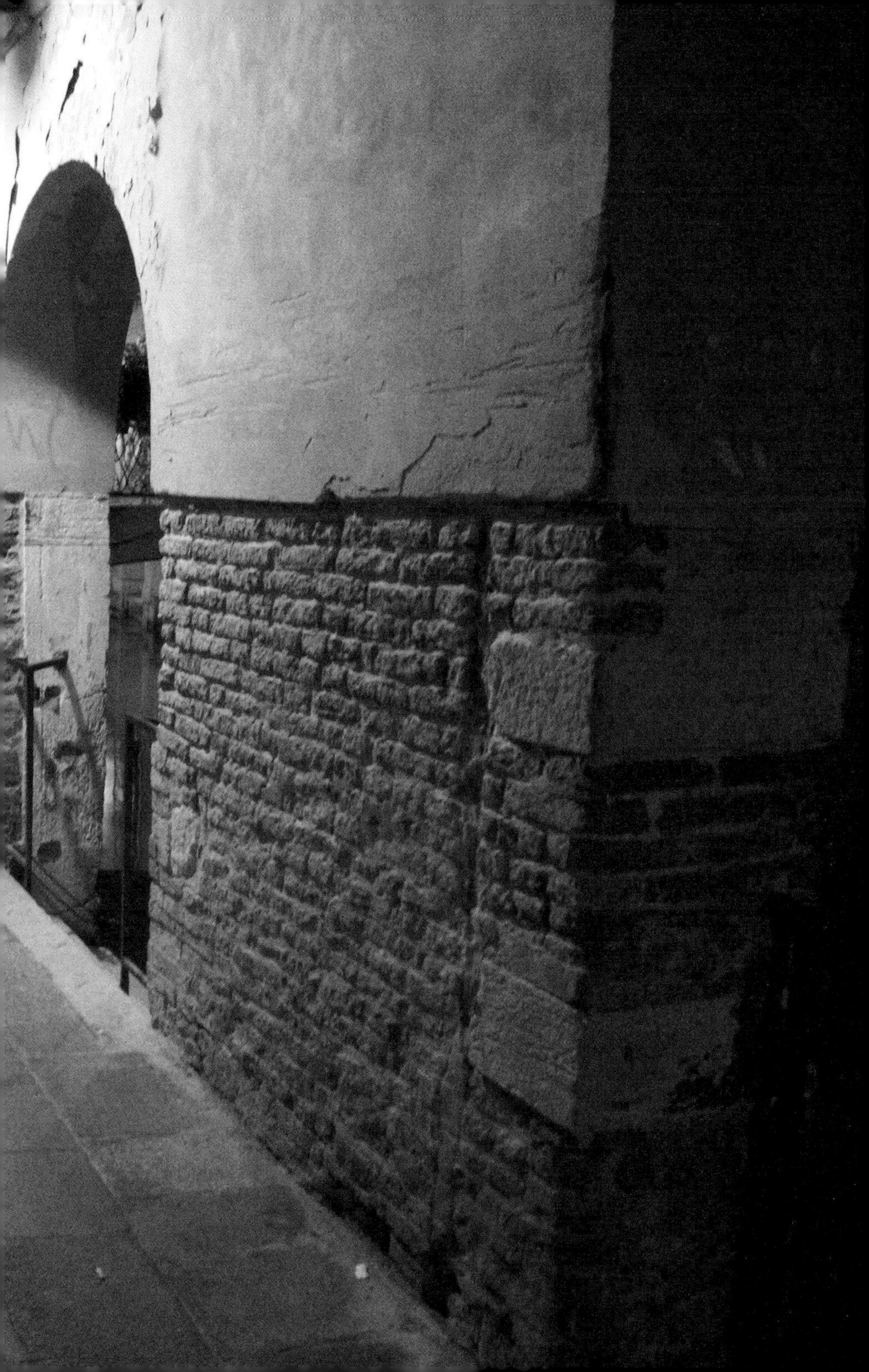

May 24th

On May 24th I set forth for Venice once again, in a mental state devoid of passion. I had nothing more in mind than to make preparations for the exhibition. Prior to that, I had been somewhat uneasy over Wu Shanzhuan's and Zhang Peili's installations, for which the material and technical requirements had led to budget increases and time pressure. In other words, no matter how lovely the scenery was, it could not overcome my anxiety and edginess. After all, a work of art that still has not taken physical form can hardly stir one's feelings or bring delight, even though the artistic impulse may be seen as a precondition for art to become a reality. I have to admit that thoughts about the exhibition did not stir the slightest passion in me. Just as I wash my face and rinse my mouth upon arising each morning, my actions were directed by a procedure or timetable. Regardless of the exhibition's importance or content, it would have to open on time. It was up to me to complete this project that needed to be completed.

<h1 style="text-align:center">5月24日</h1>

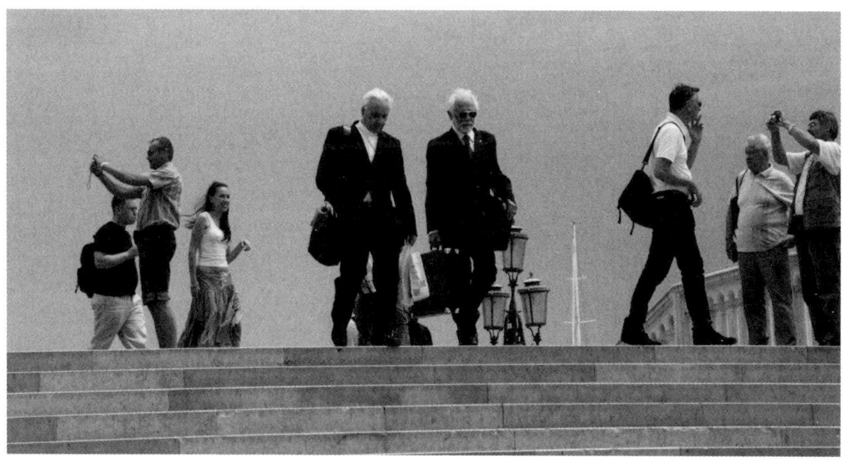

5月24日，我是在没有任何激情的心理状态下启程再次来到威尼斯的，仅仅是要为展览作提前的准备。之前，吴山专和张培力的装置作品让我心里不安，他们的作品所需要的材料与工程技术要求，导致预算的增加和时间的急迫。想说的是，没有什么"美丽的"风景能够覆盖内心的焦虑与烦躁，尤其是，没有任何艺术在成为物理事实之前能够让人激动与欢欣，尽管冲动，尤其是艺术家的内心冲动被认为是艺术之所以成为艺术的前提。因此我要承认，展览本身丝毫也没有让我有任何激情，就像我们每天清晨从床上起来需要漱口和洗脸一样，只有程序与时间表在指挥行动，无论展览是否重要，是什么性质，都需要按时开幕，我要去完成这个似乎必须去完成的项目。

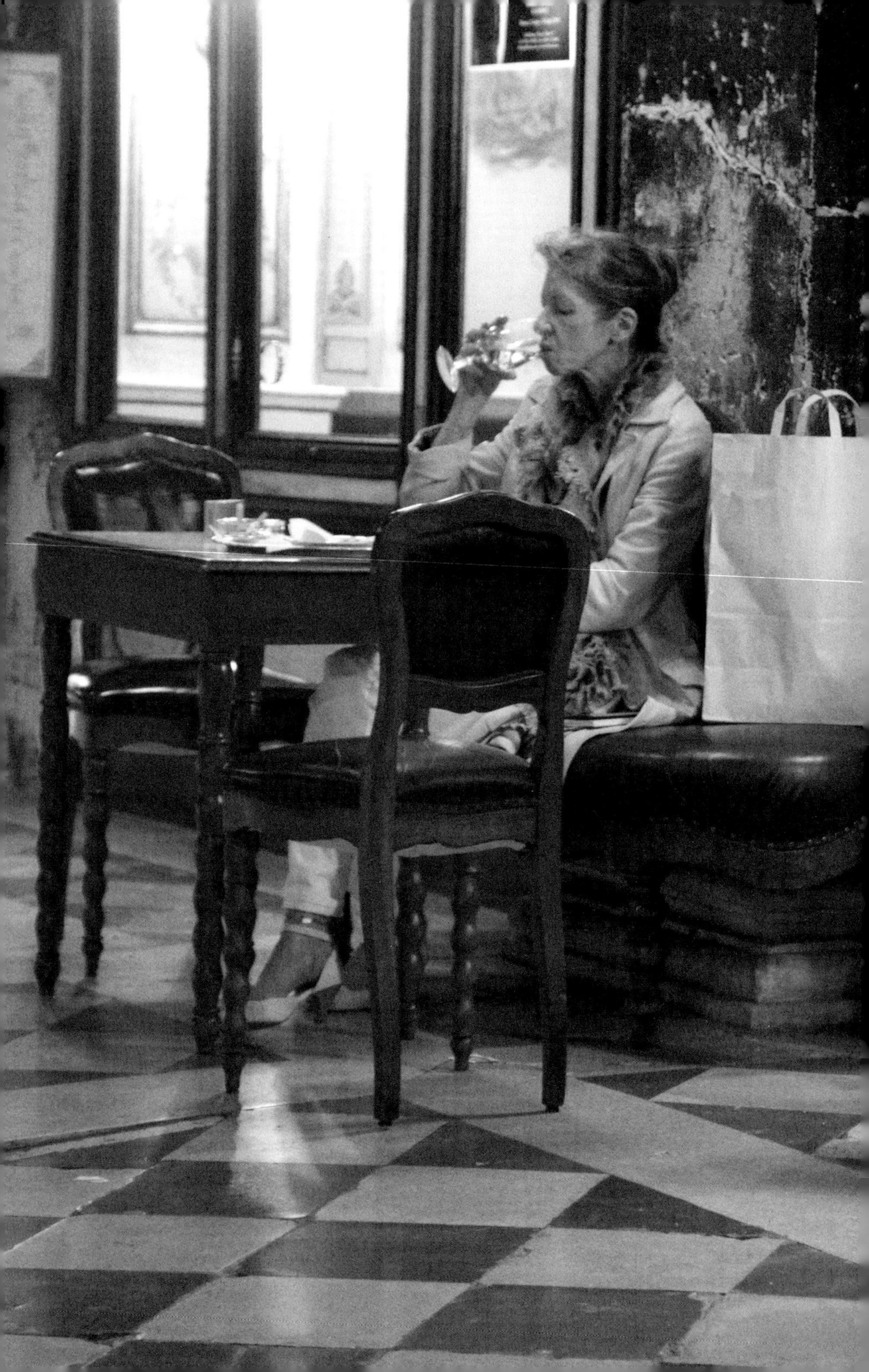

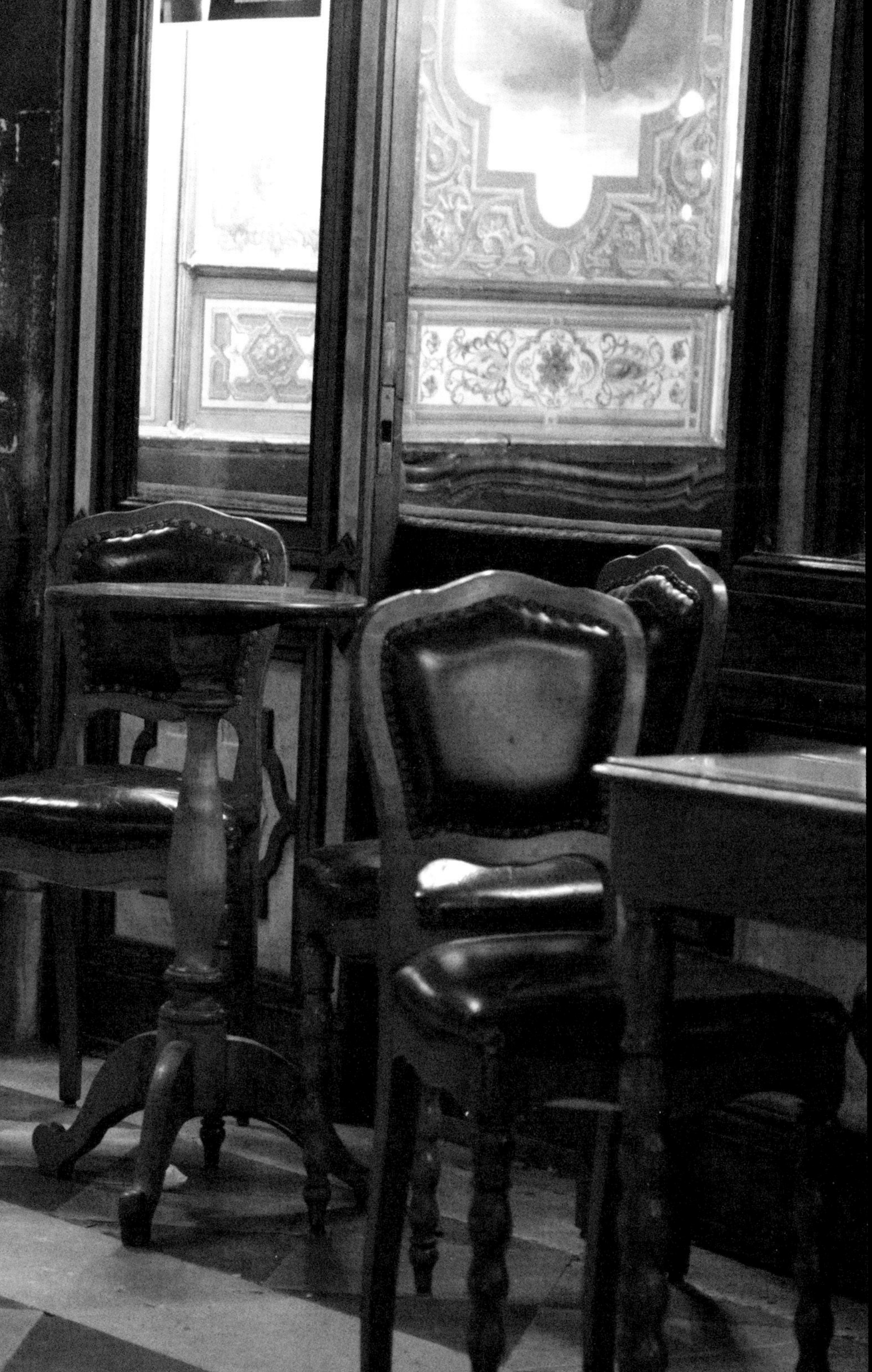

Up until the 25th, my routine offered little in the way of drama. Together with Wu Shanzhuan, Inga Svala Thórsdóttir, the designer Yin Jiulong, and his assistant, I stepped off a plane onto a rolling stairway at Marco Polo Airport, then proceeded by water taxi to San Servolo. There was nothing worth mentioning that evening, except that I heard a status report from my student Kong Liwen, who had come a few days earlier to get things underway. Nightfall came after 9:30, and we found our way to Building 19 by the glow of streetlamps. From the window we could see the darkened island, with a few lights in sight beyond a brick courtyard wall, and beyond that the ocean depths. I took another look at the courtyard in front of the church and decided that this space, with its ancient statues, would make a good site for our opening. Then we passed through the courtyard to the rear yard of the church, to check the engineers' work on Wu and Inga's installation. Standing on the scaffold ready for neon lights to be mounted, we viewed the ocean surface and the island's lights. The back of the church was set off by an expanse of shimmering reflections. At such a time, ordinary judgment would pronounce the view beautiful, but the work itself was a tense grind, and worrisome matters preyed on my mind. That was how things were. Beauty in the absence of goals and effectiveness had little to recommend it at the moment. Beauty had nothing that could induce reverie, being simply a part of the physical world. I remembered reading books by Immanuel Kant twen-

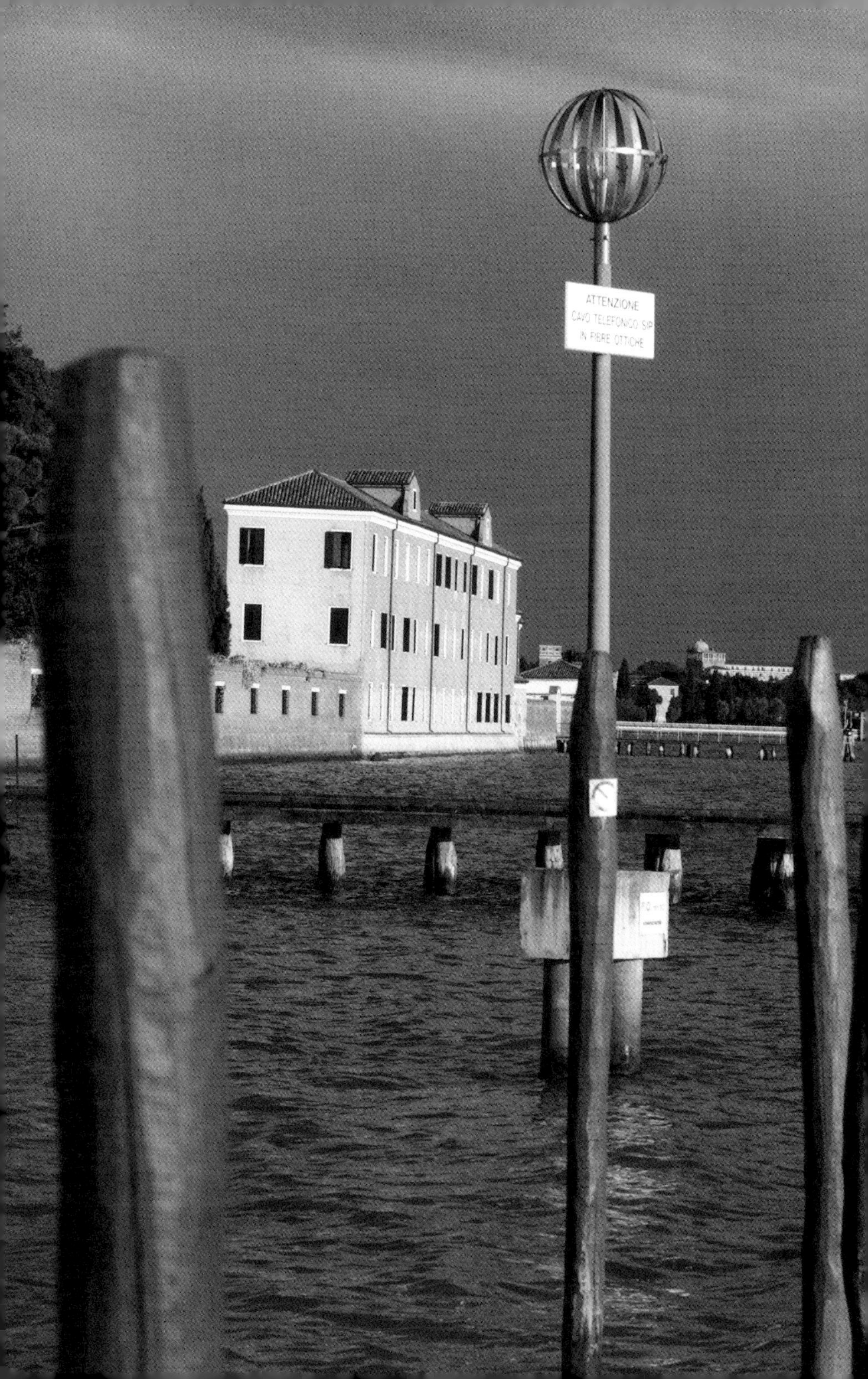

ATTENZIONE
CAVO TELEFONICO SIP
IN FIBRE OTTICHE

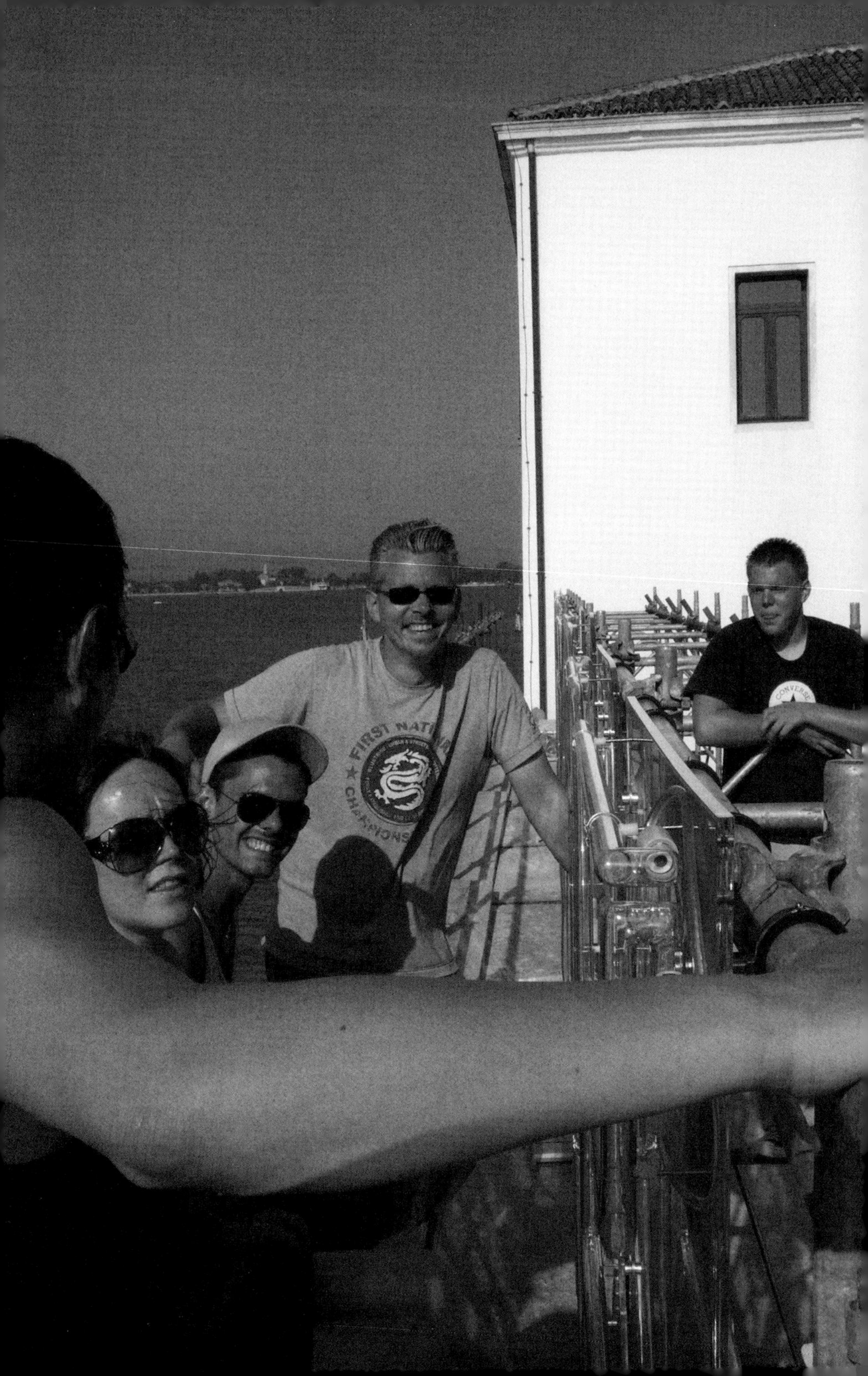

5月25日

直到25号，生活本身并没有提示任何戏剧性。我与吴山专、英嘎 (Inga Svala Thórsdóttir) 设计师殷九龙和他的助手走下飞机旋梯，我们到达了马可波罗机场。 water taxi 将我们一行送到了 San Servolo, 没有任何值得提及的事情，除了听取先前到达开展工作的学生孔立雯的工作报告。夜晚在9点半之后降临了，14号楼的路灯指示着我们，让我们领略黑夜中的 San Servolo 以及红砖墙外远处的灯光与无底的海水。我又一次观察了教堂前面的院子，我决定将这个有古代雕塑的院子作为 opening night 的场地，此外，我们要通过院子到教堂的后院去关心吴山专的工程师的工作。站在准备安装霓虹灯的脚手架上，我们眺望了海面和本岛上的灯光，波光粼粼，灯光投射出教堂的"后背"。这时，通常的感受会给出"美"的评价，不过，工作本身是枯燥的、紧张的、担心的甚至是恐惧的，情况往往就是这样，美如果离开了目的和效用，也变得不那么美了。她没有让人有任何遐想，仅仅是一处物理世界。记得20多年前，读到康德 (Immanuel Kant) 的书，很多人有了"无目的性"这个概念，我们被告知，功利与目的是有害的。人的高级精神具有抽象性，美，朝着无限的高处上升而展开。可是，在夜晚，如果我们走过灯光幽暗的教堂回廊，想到的仍然是白天现实生活中的很多麻烦事，心情仍然是下降的。没有什么精神是一直朝着抽象而去的，尽管人到终了会有抽象的意象。经常的感受就是这样，学术或者哲学的唠叨没有减弱现实的焦虑，在离开北京的前一天晚上，黄专在"梧桐"谈到了苏格拉底 (Socrates) 对"抽象"的坚持及其意义，他用"硬问题"来表述这样的坚持是何等的有价值。是的，我们向往那样的世界，好像艺术也具有实现这类向往的可能，可是，为什么人类数千年来没有达成哪怕是抽象的一致性呢？即便两个卿卿我我的情人，只

ty years before, when many people entertained the idea of "non-purposiveness." We were told that utilitarian aims were harmful, that the advanced activity of spirit was abstract and beautiful—that it unfolded and rose to unbounded heights. But our mood was subdued as we breathed the night air and walked along the church's faintly lit portico, our minds occupied with real-life hassles that would greet us in the daytime. No spiritual state can be oriented indefinitely toward abstract things, even though one will eventually conceive of abstract forms. This is what we feel at ordinary times: our real-life anxiety is not lessened by scholarly, philosophical pronouncements. On the evening before I left Beijing, Huang Zhuan had chatted at the "Scholartree" about Socrates' dedicated pursuit of "the abstract"; Huang had spoken of this as a "rigorous issue" to indicate the value of such persistence. True, we long for such a world, and it would seem that art has the potential to turn these longings into reality. But why, over the past few thousand years, has humankind not arrived at a consistency of views, at least in the abstract? Even between a pair of infatuated lovers, clashes and conflicts can arise for the slightest reasons. Two learned intellectuals can exchange views on every subject, but reality can easily deliver a blow that will split them apart. We are entities possessing a soul—if we still believe that such a term can still be pressed into use. We know that the soul is intangible, active, hard to control, hard to evade, and perhaps wholly sovereign. All things can be rendered up by the soul, including those "rigorous issues" spoken of by Huang Zhuan. Yet intellect is all too powerless and vulnerable: once confronted with troubles of the physical world, even the view of a woman's back can throw one's mind into turmoil. Although the sun's rays outside may be brilliant, much of the world is caught in a dark predicament. On top of this, I would have to begin the next morning dealing with trivial matters regarding the exhibition. Such was my mood that night.

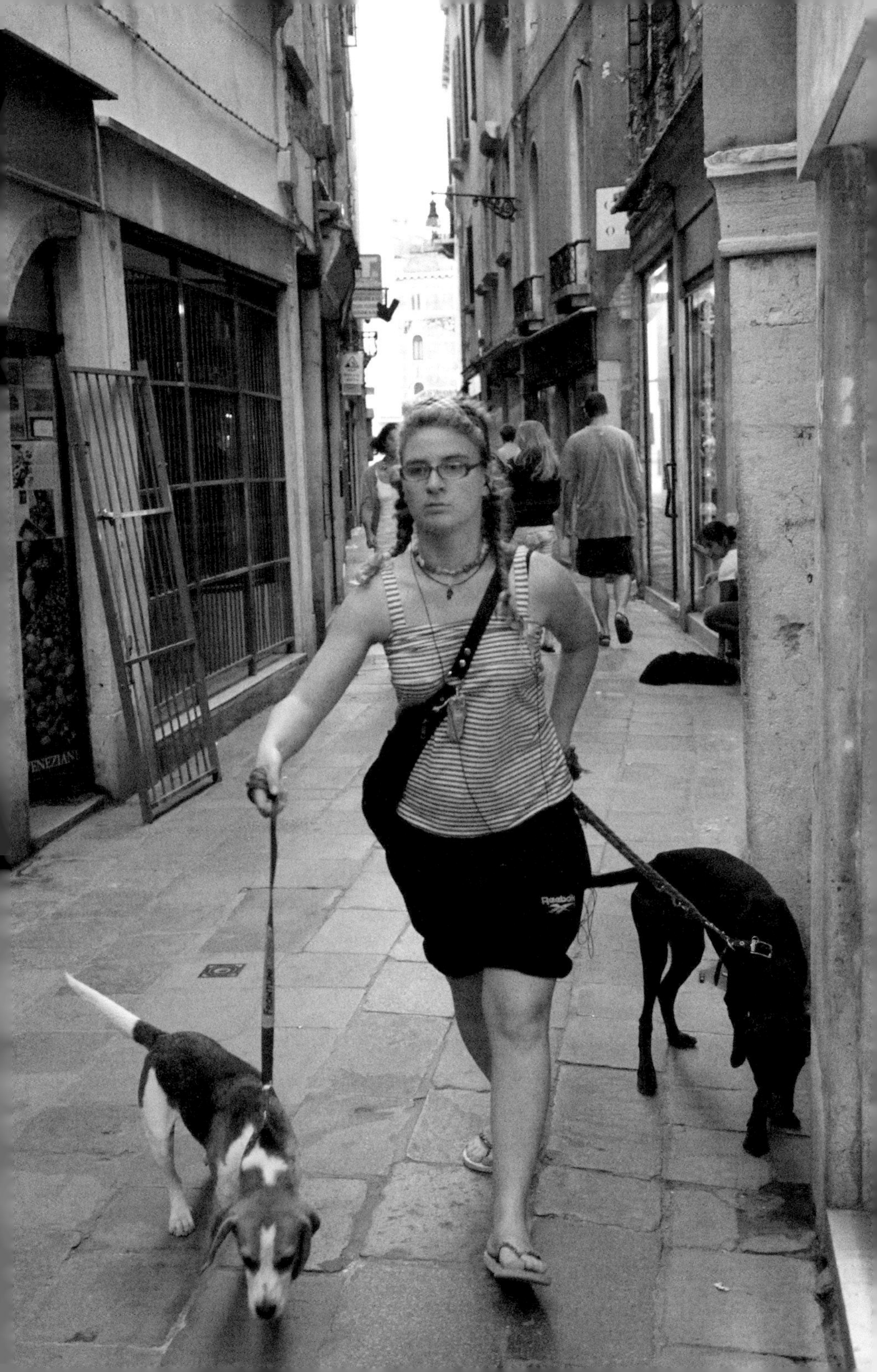

Experience told me that aside from certain people who contemplate and savor time on a microcosmic scale, few emotions are worthy of being retained indefinitely in memory. Momentary perceptions have a negligible existence, for in daily life we merely link up the matters that seem to be important, omitting everything else in between. How much can we really hold in memory? Every person holds onto something different. After a long time, we begin to feel that life does not have a great deal of content. But early in the morning, if one savors all that San Servolo has to offer, if one follows a footpath and climbs an observation deck, if one rubs a banister weathered by countless storms and gazes at marks of time upon these buildings, one realizes that the true content of memory lies in details. Details belong to the physical world. It is always through details of the physical world that we piece together our values. We say that architecture is grand, or stylish, or exquisite in taste, but we are talking about things in the physical world. We speak of Venice's beauty, which is composed of alleyways of varying widths, of flowing water, of boats and multicolored processions of people. All of these things pertain to the physical world. We listen to music beside a verandah at Piazza San Marco. We drink coffee while the music carries us away to a time long past—memories too are of the physical world. We think of historical figures, just as one might go to the Guggenheim Museum or the Academia and pore over a work by Titian. We imagine stories that may have happened behind a small time-mottled door in an alley. We imagine experiences of passersby on the street. As we stand on Rialto Bridge and watch the gondoliers, we may think of works by French Impressionist painters. Actually, all of these things pertain to the physical world. When you are no longer in this world, will there not be other lovers passing through these winding canals? Of course Schopenhauer reminds us that the world is a representation of our awareness. The importance of awareness has been evoked in countless

要一丝原因，冲突和矛盾就油然而生；两个有智慧的知识分子讨论学术问题，也很容易被现实的一击而导致分离。我们是灵魂构成的——如果我们认可"灵魂"或者"spirit"这样的词汇仍然可以勉强使用的话，我们知道灵魂是不可捉摸的，活动的，不能控制的，不可躲避的，或者完全有自主权的，灵魂可以给出一切，包括黄专说的那些"硬问题"，可是，智慧是如此地相对无力与脆弱，只要面对物理世界给出的麻烦，一个女人离去的背影都会让你心烦意乱，世界在很多时间里处在黑暗中，尽管这里白天的阳光异常灿烂，何况我将在次日开始去解决那些有关展览的琐碎工作，这就是这个晚上我的心情。

经验告诉我们，对于那些没有将时间放在对微观世界的思考和体会上的人来说，没有什么情绪是值得或能够让记忆永久操劳的，每分每秒中的感知并不存在，在日常生活中，我们仅仅是把似乎重要的事情联系起来，而省略掉了中间的一切。我们能够记住什么？每个人都不一样。时间长了，我们会觉得我们的生活没有什么太多的内容。可是，在清晨，如果领略一下 San Servolo 的一切：走过那些小径，步上木板搭建的眺望台，抚摩被风雨抚摩过无数次的柱廊，观看建筑的那些被时间侵蚀而出现的斑驳，

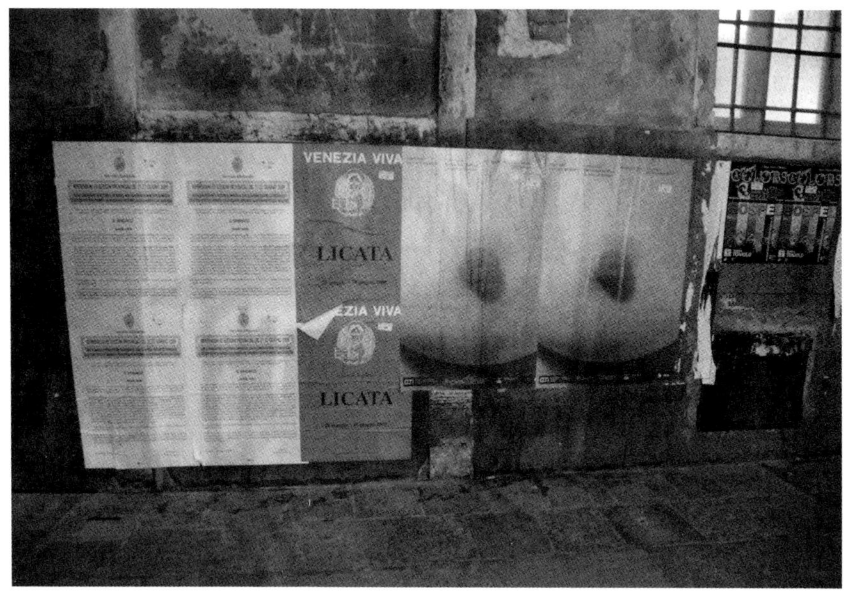

writings, but persons of experience will perhaps agree that awareness belongs likewise to the physical world, even though we are made aware of this world by our awareness.

就可以知道，只有细节才是记忆的真正内容。细节属于物理世界，我们总是通过物理世界的细节来拼凑我们的价值，我们说建筑是如何的雄伟，充满风格与绝妙的趣味，可是，我们说的都是物理世界的事情；我们讨论威尼斯的美，那也是由那些不同宽窄的小巷、流水、船只以及花花绿绿的人群构成的，这些还是物理世界的事情；我们倾听圣马可广场回廊边的音乐，我们喝咖啡，甚至我们被音乐带到遥远的过去，那也是物理世界的记忆，我们想到历史中的人物，如果你去了古根海姆美术馆，或者在 Academia 博物馆里阅读到了提香，我们想象小巷里关闭着的有时间痕迹的小门里的故事，想象迎面而来的路人的经历，当我们站在 Rialto 桥上观看 Gondola 上的船夫，也许，很快就想到了那些在法国印象主义者的作品中看到的风景，所有的这一切，其实都是物理世界的东西。当你不在这个世界上的时候，那些弯弯曲曲的水巷中就不会有别的情人？叔本华当然提醒过我们：世界就是我们感知的表象。感知的重要性被无数的文字描述过，可是，有经历的人可能会更同意：感知，似乎仍然属于物理的世界，尽管这个世界为感知所感知。

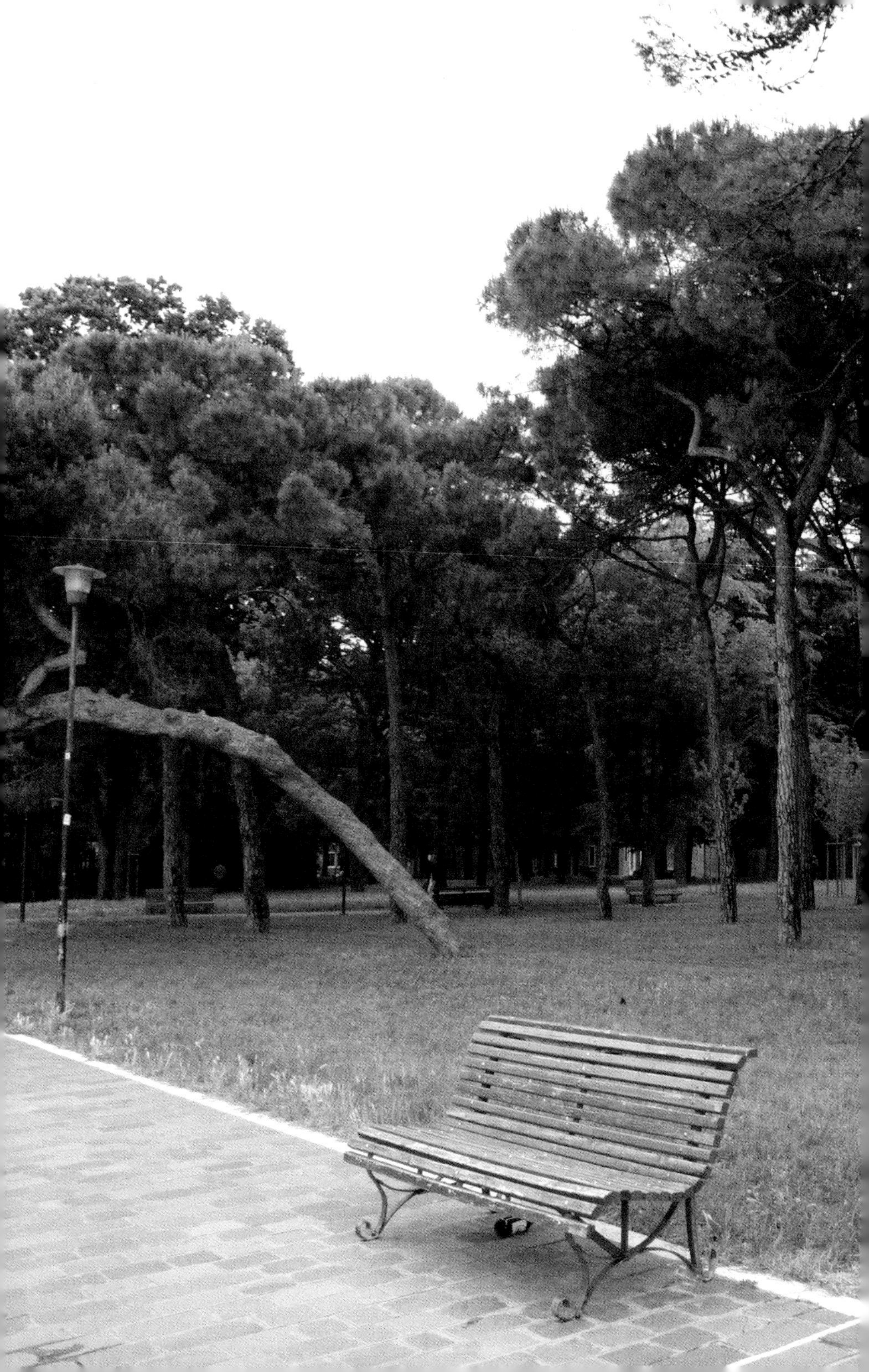

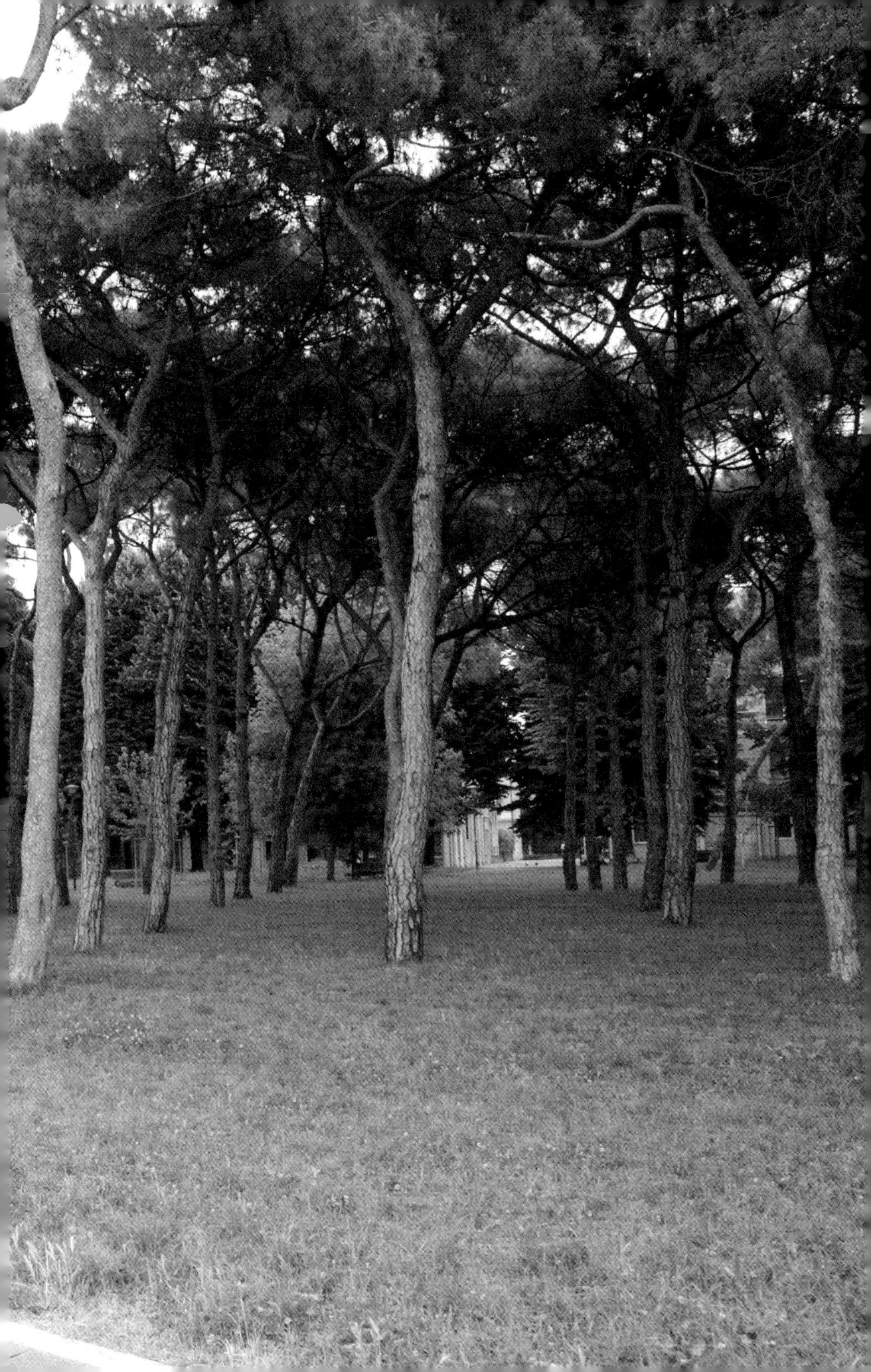

May 26th

Early in the morning on the 26th I looked out at the sea's expanse stretching from beneath my window. The just-risen sun illuminates white buildings on a small island in the distance. Is this not simply the physical world? A morning landscape like this one makes me more inclined to use words like "moved" or "touched" than any work of art. Here one might readily fall into descriptions of art and nature offered by the ancients, or one may recall judgments of many artists and thinkers regarding art and nature. I am aware that only in the past century or so has nature been neglected or viewed with disdain by some artists. Through my reading I have learned that the meaning imputed to nature has changed. We are arriving at a new understanding of nature; we have come to understand that our mental world is part of nature, or even that the mind itself is nature. Thus we often find ourselves falling back into pitfalls of philosophical language, to become prisoners of history and the ancients. When we arrived at the site of "TOBUY IS TOCREATE" (Wu insisted on this layout of English letters in his installation), the German engineer, Roger Juers, was already up on the scaffold, at work with his two sons. Usually for laborers who work in intense sunlight, there is little "beauty" in these bright rays. High temperatures prompt sweating and throw off the balance of blood metabolites, leading to instability of mood, fatigue, and tiredness. It can lead to unfocused feelings and lack of concern; it can lead to neglect of details. But things do not always play out this way in fact. Under the sun's sweltering glare, the three Germans were working

5月26日

26日的清晨，推开窗户就可以看到水临窗边的大海。刚刚升起来的太阳将她的光线投射在远处一个小岛的白色的建筑上。这可是物理世界。如果一定要使用"感动"这样的词汇，清晨的风景比艺术更让我容易使用这样的词汇。这里很可能掉进了古人对艺术和自然的描述，让我们回想到无数艺术家和哲学家关于自然的判断。我知道，也就是在一百年左右的时间，自然才被一些艺术家所忽视和轻蔑。通过读书，我知道了自然的含义已经被改变，我们在重新认识和理解自然，我们将自己的心灵世界也理解为自然中的一部分，甚至心灵就是自然。于是，我们经常发现我们回到了哲学的语词陷阱中，成为历史与古人的俘虏。当我们到了安装 TOBUY IS TOCREATE （英文的安排是吴的生造）的现场时，德国工程师已经在脚手架上工作了。通常，对于那些在烈日下工作或者劳动的人来说，阳光不是很美丽的，温度增加了汗水与内分泌紊乱的几率，导致情绪的不稳定，导致疲倦与困顿，导致对感情的不专一和不关心，导致对细节的放弃。不过，事实也不完全是这样，在炎热刺眼的阳光下，三个德国人——父亲 Roger Juers 与他的两个儿子——像机器一样一丝不苟地在这里工作。我们养成的生活态度，尤其是自由散漫的人会不接受"机器"这个词汇。它没有感性的力量，对于柔情似水的人来说，它几乎是暴力的同义词。在我到达 San Servolo 之前，我想象不出吴山专作品的脚手架和有机玻璃的字母会是怎样一种情形。然而，当我看到了那些用有机玻璃做成的字母，看到了那些精致的螺丝钉，看到了德国人在烈日下的状态，我不得不使用"很专业"这个词汇。于是，理智，或者说"机器"唤起了激情，精确与完美成为我们喜悦的依据。这是我的感受。我告诉那位父亲："你很专业。"吴山专告诉我，没有什么比"你很专业"更

like meticulous robots. We have developed a view of life—especially the easygoing, freewheeling types among us—that rejects the description "robot-like." It lacks feeling, and for those of a tender, sentimental bent, it probably sounds a bit brutal. Before arriving at San Servolo, I could not imagine what the frame and clear acrylic letters of Wu and Inga's installation would look like. When I saw the letters cut in clear acrylic being screwed accurately into place, and when I saw the Germans at work in the bright sunlight, I could think of no comment more applicable than "very professional." At times like this, rationality—or, if you like, "robot-like" qualities—can stir one's heart. Accuracy and perfection can be the basis for delight. This was what I felt, and I told the father: "You are very professional." Wu Shanzhuan told me that no comment could have brought them more joy than this. For them, being professional was a great source of pride. Everything was underway, even rough work such as hauling rubble into the exhibition space where Wang Guangyi's piece would be exhibited. Wide pieces of white fabric had to be laid out in the corridor, so that not even rubber cart tires would damage the interior floor. More workers showed up in the exhibition space to change floodlights, mount drywall, and scrape grouting. Prior to all this, while making a preliminary survey with Francesca on April 4th, I had felt a serious lack of passion on the Italian side. Instead I had sensed indifference and a lack of concern. Now the place had a look of bustling progress. That afternoon at 4:00 I went to the site of Wu and Inga's piece. Work on the installation was complete, and the German engineer was lounging on the grass, smoking and drinking colas with his sons. Neon tubes had been mounted precisely inside the clear acrylic letters. The technical work that had concerned me was now finished: at this point a coat of white paint could be applied to the installation's frame. This was my strongest impression on May 26th: "robot-like" progress, professionalism, and verve. At twilight we dined together outside the cafeteria. I took a picture of the German engineer at twilight and later uploaded the photo to

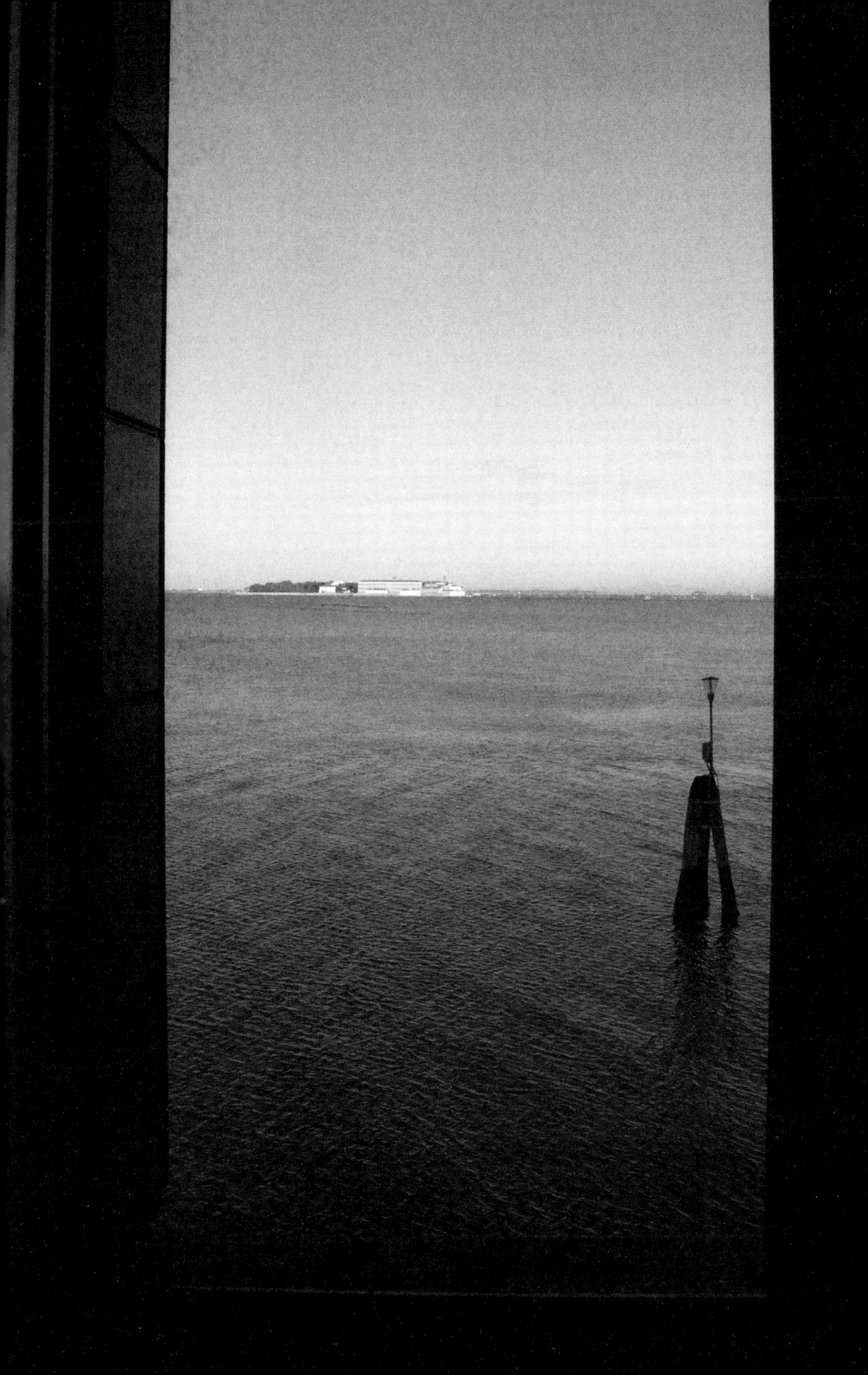

the web. This was my gesture of respect for the German spirit. In the art scene back in China, within the field of technical work, I had rarely seen such excellent quality and attitude.

In my discussions with Wu Shanzhuan, we often stressed the idea of "independence" and its function. Though I knew the importance of language, I wondered how one could go about proving the power of language in a physical way. Whether or not I agreed with it, I would persist in my vigilance toward words. In many situations, words possess no power or influence. This is a matter of issues involving "referent" vis-à-vis "subjective reference," as philosophers or linguists might put it. In fact, when using a sign to convey an idea, our aim is to have an influence. In conveying thoughts to other people, what most concerns us is physical influence. In 1992 I became fed up with the tenuousness of metaphysics and even came to see it as a smokescreen for deception. I found myself wanting to conduct disgusting "manipulations," as a response to the vagueness of words and their beautiful indefiniteness. To be frank, power in a physical sense is what gives me a feeling of strength and influence. That was seventeen years ago, before I had read the works of Foucault, though his works were on my shelf. Looking back today, I can see that the motivating force for every philosopher and thinker comes from his particular context. I do not believe that Foucault understood our context, although he believed he understood the general context of human discourse. Critics and artists focusing on others' work often evaluate exhibitions with phrases like "it would seem" or "one could say." Yet in many cases they lack a grasp of the artist's context. They prefer to believe in their own perspicuity. But when they take leave of the other person's context, problems of understanding will arise. As a result, their words end up having little effect, and may even increase discord and conflict. My delight on the evening of the 26th did not come from words, inasmuch as Wu Shanzhuan had hatched the concept of this phrase way back in 1992. What is more, he had exhibited the semantic equivalent in Chinese characters—"*mai*

能够让他们感到幸福与愉快的了，他们为"专业"而感到无比骄傲与自豪。一切都在进行中，即便是非常粗的活路，例如将废土拉进展览空间——那是王广义的作品空间，也有一个宽宽的白色织物被安排在走廊，目的就是让即便是橡胶做的轮子也不要损坏了室内的地面。更多的工人出现在展览空间，拆卸壁灯，安装镶板，将膏灰刮在镶板上。之前，那是我在4月25日到 San Servolo 与 Francesca 研究工作的时候，我感受到的是意大利方激情与紧张的严重欠缺，甚至只有没有太多关心的冷漠。现在，这里的一

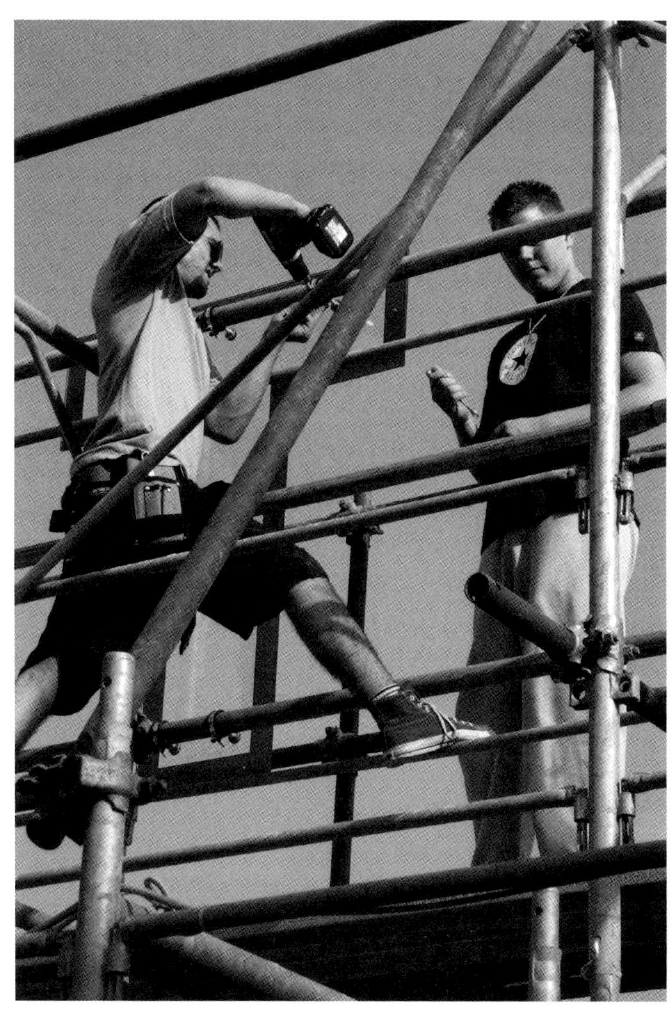

jiushi chuang"—in 2005, at a show curated by Gao Shiming in Hangzhou. My delight on the evening of the 26th came from the concrete, physical world. It came from professional attitude and intelligence. It came from labor under scorching sunlight; it came from the world that is available to our eyes and hands. As we sat in the courtyard on San Servolo, Wu's words were facing away from us. What I saw at twilight was the backside of a phrase.

Imagine what it must have been like for Marco Polo, his uncle, and his son as they traveled to the "great capital" 800 years ago. They were beset by storms and armed conflicts along the way. A big part of their original intent was the quest for wealth, and there are no sources indicating that they sought anything immaterial. In his *Travels*, the stories that Marco Polo relates all happen in the physical world. Yet those stories prompted countless Europeans to travel to the "Orient" too, to seek out all the forms of interchange this world allows. We believe in the power of spirit, but we are apt to overlook spirit's role in physical, instinctual activity. When Marco Polo opened his chest of treasures to show his townsmen, it was his "fortune" that attracted people's attention and earned their trust. This sounds vulgar, and scholars have raised questions of authenticity, so some people may even relegate Marco Polo to the realm of "myth." But when we arrived again at Marco Polo Airport, and when we saw a boat named Marco Polo, and when we saw the name Marco Polo in various places around the city, we were reminded of the power of the physical world. Wu Shanzhuan had no interest in holding a dialogue with Marco Polo, but "to buy is to create" was surely an intention shared by Marco Polo. The merchant families of Venice believed that miracles could be attained through commercial interchange. These families did indeed create a miracle, and that is enough. Now Wu Shanzhuan had restated Marco Polo's aim in writing and posted it on a small island in Marco Polo's native place. What could be a more earnest, sacred act of respect for the miracle Marco Polo created?

切都显示出开始与进步。下午4点半，当我再次走到吴山专作品的现场，安装工作已经结束，德国父子三人已经在草地上抽烟和喝着可乐，霓虹灯已经十分精确地被安装在了有机玻璃的字母板上，让我最担心的工程最早完成了，这时，张培力的安装现场才出现了白色的涂料。这是我在26日中最深的印象："机器"与进步，专业与快乐。黄昏，我们在食堂的外边共进晚餐。我把一张父亲在黄昏中的照片挂在了网上，是想表达对德国精神的敬意，在国内艺术圈的工作范围里，我几乎没有看到过这样的工作态度和质量。

我与吴山专经常讨论的是词语的独立性及其作用，尽管我们知道语言的重要性，可是，语言的物理力量在什么时候可以得到证明？无论是否同意，我坚持对语词保持警惕，在很多情况下，语词并不具备力量与影响力。这倒不完全是因为哲学家和语言学家使用了"能指"与"所指"及其变化中的问题这类表述的原因，事实上，我们用一种符号和方式去表达一个概念，目的在于产生影响，将需要传达的意思传达给他人，影响的物理作用是我们最关心的事情。我在1992年就厌倦了形而上学的飘渺甚至觉得其中隐藏着的蒙骗，我希望用让人感到可恶的"操作"来回应语词的模糊性与美妙的不确定性。坦诚地说，是物理意义上的权力让我感受到力量和影响力的。那是十七年前的事情，我没有阅读过福柯（Michel Foucault）的著作，尽管他的书已经在我的书架上。今天想来，每个哲学家和思想家的思想动因都来自他的特殊语境，我相信，福柯不了解我们的语境，尽管他相信他了解人类的上下文。批评家和关注别人的艺术家经常要对他们看到的展览评头论足："假如"，"如果"，"要是"，这样的词汇很多，可是，一般的情况是，他们对于别人具体的工作并不十分了解，他们宁可相信自己的正确性和智慧。在这个时候，他们脱离了别人特殊的语境，理解出现了问题，结果，语词没有起到太多的作用，也许，更加加强了歧义与冲突。26日的夜晚所拥有的惬意不是来自语词，因为吴山专的"语词"早在1992年的某一天就被他发现了，并且，2005年，我在杭州看到了他的"买就是创造"的中文字出现在高士明策划的展览上。26日的夜晚所拥有的惬意来自具体的物理世界，来自专业的态度与智慧，来自烈日下的劳动，来自我们的眼睛和手能够感觉到的世界。吴的"语词"背对着我们，在 San Servolo 的院子里，在黄昏里，我们只能看到语

Lights of a city at night may be filled with warmth, if only one has a warm heart.

Chinese people soon began referring to San Servolo as "Crazy Man Island," conveying their hard-to-pin-down feelings about the place. What a fine nickname! Before long there would be more "crazy people" from China convening here to carry on this island's traditions. By this point we had recovered metaphysics; we had recovered affection and emotion. This was a night of elation, a night we could devote to observing our psychic world, because "craziness" is nothing other than metaphysics.

词的背影。

想象一下800年前 Marco Polo 父、叔、子三人在前往"大都"路上的情景，风雨交加，战事频仍，他们的初衷的很大一部分是为了寻求财富，同时，没有资料表明他们寻求的财富不是物质财富。在 Marco Polo 的《游记》(*The Travels*) 里，他所描述的所有故事都是在物理世界发生的事。然而，那些故事影响了以后无数的欧洲人前往"东方"，寻求物理世界中的所有沟通。我们相信精神的力量，却很容易忽视精神作为本能的物理运动，当Marco Polo在他的乡亲面前打开他的财宝时，是所谓的"百万"吸引了人们的关注并赢得了人们最后的信任。这听上去很俗气，再加上学者的怀疑，人们甚至可以将 Marco Polo 的"神话"置之不理，可是，当我们再次到达 Marco Polo 机场，再次看到印有Marco Polo字母的船只，再次四处可见 Marco Polo 的名字时，我们发现了物理世界本身的力量。吴山专并没有兴趣与 Marco Polo对话，可是， to buy is to create 也一定是 Marco Polo 的意思，威尼斯商人家族相信在买卖的沟通中将会获得奇迹，他们一家人已经创造出了奇迹，这已经够了。现在，吴山专将 Marco Polo 的目的再次写出来，挂在 Marco Polo 的故乡的小岛上，这是对 Marco Polo 创造的奇迹最礼貌、最神圣的敬意。

夜晚的灯光充满温情，如果我们有一颗温情的心

San Servolo 很快被国内的人怀着难以名状心情简称为"疯人岛"，这是多么好的称谓。很快，将有更多来自中国的"疯人"聚集在这里，实现这个岛的传承。现在，我们恢复了形而上学，恢复了温情以及感性。正是惬意的夜晚，让我们开始有重点地观察自己的精神世界，因为"疯"就是形而上学。

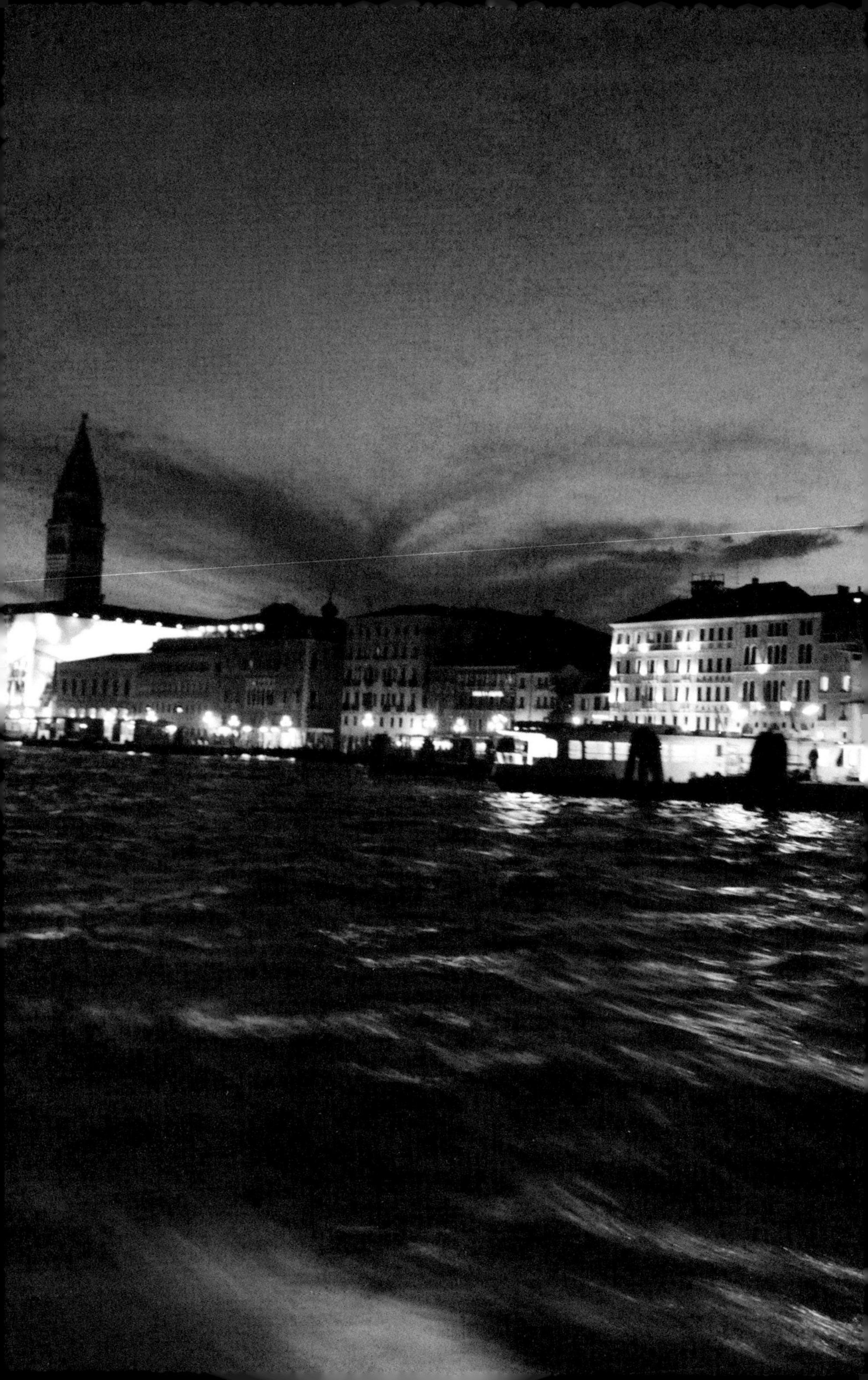

May 27th

The morning of the 27th was overcast, and that was when Zhang Peili arrived. "Crazy Man Island" had been awaiting the arrival of yet another crazy man. This crazy man's works came from the ocean of his subconscious. He intended to give Hangzhou's "Piazza San Marco" back to the Venetians. Interestingly, his planned present to Marco Polo was a repeatedly inflating and deflating Tower of Piazza San Marco. In order to make the tower puff up and shrivel convincingly, he had to deal with tedious adjustment procedures and tense manipulations.

That evening we rode a water taxi rented by Inga to view the neon light effects. The university's floodlights helped bring out "Crazy Man Island's" beauty and mystery. The water sparkled with rippling reflections, and there was a slight nip in the air. The words "TOBUY IS TOCREATE" cast long gleaming shapes over the waves, combining with faint reflections of buildings to make an aqueous night scene. The red neon gave me a sense of warmth. The boat headed toward Piazza San Marco—we wanted to view the installation's effect from a distance. One can discover beauty in a night view of sparkling lights, but this may be altered by one's nighttime mood. Actually, loneliness is part of what the sparkling lights evoke, when one thinks of friends who are not in happy circumstances, or thinks of time frittered away, or thinks of all that begins and fades in a sparkling interval, or thinks of one's youthful ideals and vows, or thinks of promises to oneself and of how all things are swallowed up at night—hidden, ignored, put out of mind. The boat's course took it mid-water, far from any

5月27日

27日上午的天空有很多乌云，那是张培力到达的时间，"疯人岛"等待着另一个"疯人"的即将到达。这个"疯人"的作品来自无意识的海洋，他要将在杭州的 Piazza San Marco 送还给威尼斯人，最有趣的是，他决定将一个不断充气挺直又不断瘪气的 Tower of Piazza San Marco 送给 Marco Polo。为了让这个塔能够很好地坚挺与收缩，他将面临枯燥的调试与长时间的操作焦虑。

晚上，我们乘着英噶租来的 water taxi，去观看霓虹灯的效果。学校的景观灯让"疯人岛"呈现出夜晚的神秘与美丽，波光粼粼，有些寒气。而 TOBUY IS TOCREATE 已经在海面上印出了闪烁的波光，与隐隐约约的建筑倒影构成了新的夜景，红色的霓虹灯给了我们暖意。船朝圣马可广场方向开去——我们希望在远处眺望作品的效果。灯光闪烁的夜晚本来可以是美的，然而，在黑夜里的心情可能将这一切改变。事实上，孤独也是闪烁中的内容，想想那些并不欢乐的朋友，想想时间的蹉跎，想想一切都在闪烁中开始和消失，想想青春时期的理想与愿望，想想自己对自己的承诺，一切都像黑夜里的物，被吞噬，被隐去，被忽略，被抛弃。当船只游行在远离岸边的水中央时，岸上的一切并不具有吸引力，他们或者它们仅仅是冷漠的思考的对象，芸芸众生、来来回回、周而复始，都可以是描述岸边的词汇。我们就是中间的一员，是来来回回、周而复始的内容之一，可是，我们在黑夜里也可以观察我们自己，在移动的建筑、移动的灯光和移动的人群中，我们很容易感受到消失与离去。不过，吴山专和英噶在船尾却表现出温馨的状态与情绪，这是男女构成的局部世界，他们看到他们的作品已经成就，他们感到快乐与高兴。大千世界就是这样构成的，所有的景致没有好坏，是我们的心情投射的结果。所谓的"美"也不过是心情的投射而已。对于那些远离他乡

bank, until all that was ashore held no attraction, until things and people became only objects of cold, detached thought. "Milling crowd"…"coming and going"…"meandering about"… All these phrases aptly describe life back on the shore. Each of us is just one player, one element in what is described as a "milling crowd." But in the dark night, as buildings slide by, as crowds and lights drift by, we can observe ourselves. At such times it is easy to feel ourselves fading away and departing. However, Wu Shanzhuan and Inga, back in the boat's stern, were having a moment of tender affection. This was their world within a world, composed of the two sexes. They saw that their creative work had been accomplished, and they were glad. Of such pieces is the world of worlds comprised. Each presents a vista, in which there is no good or bad except as a projection of one's own mood. What is called beauty is no more than a projection of our mood. For those who have left their native place and who are concerned for loved ones, lovers, and friends, exotic scenes of another land have only fleeting beauty. In other words, warm lamplight and rippling reflections may not lead to elation and may in fact lead to forlornness. I can only surmise that the night was beautiful and delightful to my students Kong Liwen and Zhao Na. (Yet my surmise may be inaccurate, because I cannot know their inner feelings at that moment.)

Again I plunged into a routine morning. Ample sunlight beamed down on the area outside the cafeteria; the sky was a perfect blue. Tranquil San Servolo was bright but lacking in anything one could describe enthusiastically. After checking on the progress of work at the exhibition site, I sat down in the V.I.U. coffee shop with Wu and Zhang. We talked about the history of Zhejiang Fine Arts Institute since the 1980s. We talked about why nearly all the people at Zhe-Arts have gotten into conceptual art: Huang Yongbing, Gu Wenda, Wu Shanzhuan, Zhang Peili, and Wang Guangyi. Of course our discussion also touched on Geng Jianyi. In the past few years this kind of discussion has come up frequently. I wondered if this meant that a great deal

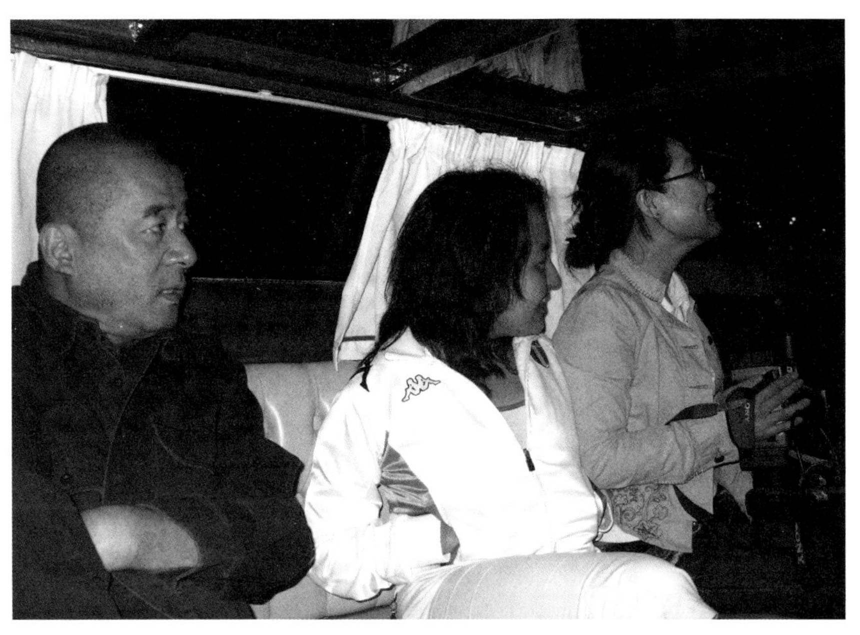

而又有亲人、情人、爱人、朋友挂念的人来说，往往，即便是看到异国他乡的风景，美是不多的，转瞬即逝的。换句话说，温暖的灯光或者粼粼波光不一定导致惬意，倒可能引起凄迷。我仅仅是猜测，对于船上的学生孔立雯和赵娜来说，这个夜晚可能是新奇的和美丽的，因而是惬意的（尽管我的猜测可能并不准确，因为我不知道她们此刻的内心）。

再次进入一个重复的早晨，阳光将食堂外的环境照射得非常充分，天空蓝蓝，安静的 San Servolo 在此刻只有明亮但缺乏描述内容的风光。在检查了展览现场的工作进展之后，吴、张和我在VIU的咖啡厅的室外坐下来。我们讨论了"浙美"的历史（当然是80年代以来的），讨论了为什么"浙美"的人几乎都是观念主义者：黄永砯、谷文达、吴山专、张培力、王广义，我们当然也讨论到了耿建翌。在最近几年，这样的讨论不时出现，这是否意味着时间已经过去很多，人正在变得老去？也许这不是一个感伤的表述，而是时间的自然提醒，但是，这都差不多，经历就是时间，一旦太多，就是堆积，人会自然而然地去想起。

理解艺术是永远的话题，可是，人们对艺术的不同理解导致

of time had gone by and we were getting old. Perhaps this was not a foreboding sign but simply a natural reminder of time. Yet one might just as well be the other. Experience is equivalent to time: once there is too much of it, one begins to think of it as mere deposition.

Understanding art is an eternal topic, but people understand art in different ways and this can lead to long stretches of perplexity. Our discussion clearly had a particular context. Beginning in 2006 people in the art scene began discussing art of the 1980s extensively, up until the chaotic, deplorable year of 2008, when invective against supposedly successful artists began to appear on the web. San Servolo was a good place for us to discuss art calmly, being far away from the noise back in China. In this sense, this "Crazy Man Island" was more like a serene paradise where we could sort out our worldly disputes.

Most Chinese people know something about the "Seven Sages of the Bamboo Grove." Under the radiant sun, Wu Shan-zhuan once again brought up this concept about intellectuals from Chinese history. I don't claim to be highly familiar with the biographical details of these seven figures, and I prefer to think of them loosely as standing for a temperament or attitude. I think of their ethos of human behavior, or of their spiritual quality that sets them apart from worldly hubbub. Although there is a plethora of writing about contemporary art on the web, it has little or no meaning for today's "Seven Sages of the Bamboo Grove." Actualities have impressed upon us that exchanges of words are incapable of bringing about true communication or communion among people. As for people who are able to communicate, who are in communion, do they really need an exchange of words? We know that they do not. They merely need wine, women, and enlightenment. Western thinkers naturally emphasize rationality, but for Chinese people, enlightenment or experiential insight are most important. Time is passing, moment by moment: unless one is doing good deeds, there is no point in spending time on people with whom one cannot communicate. Jean-Paul

了对艺术持久的困惑。我们的谈话显然有一个特殊的语境，从2006年以来，艺术圈的人们开始更多地谈论80年代的艺术历史，直到混乱而糟糕的2008年，网上终于开始对那些被认为成功的艺术家展开批评或者咒骂。远离国内的喧嚣的 San Servolo 是个好地方，她让我们可以很安静地去讨论艺术。从这个意义上讲，这个"疯人岛"更像一个平静的天堂乐园，可以供我们清理人世间的问题。

中国人大都熟悉"竹林七贤"的故事。在灿烂的阳光下，吴山专再次提及到了这个关于历史上的中国知识分子的概念。我并不认为我很熟悉这七个人的所有事迹，而宁可将这个概念看成是一种气质和态度，看成是一个做人的标准，甚至看成是一个脱离喧嚣的精神空气。尽管网上有太多关于当代艺术的文字，对于今天的"竹林七贤"来说，没有丝毫的意义。许多事实让我们感受到，语词之间的交流无法实现任何沟通与共鸣。那些能够沟通和拥有共鸣的人真的需要语词吗？不是，我们知道，他们仅仅需要酒、女人与领悟。西方思想家当然注重"理性"，而对于中国人来说，"领悟"与"体会"是最重要的。时间每分钟都在流逝，除非你在实施善的行为，否则不应该将时间用在不能沟通的人那里。萨特（Jean-Paul Sartre）的"他人就是地狱"的内涵可以改写，至少可以表述为"他人就是消耗"，否则，那些无意识的声音将销蚀你的能量以及智慧，沟通没有可能性，为什么还要去努力去沟通呢？对话没有可能性为什么要去对话呢？时间一直都在告诉我们谜底：时间本身就是答案。所以，吴山专终于说出来："其实，关于世界（艺术），就是三五个人之间的认可、沟通与交流就可以了。准确地讲，我们只在意少数人之间的恐慌或友情。"张培力表示了对批评家使用概念的反感，他几乎不相信语词本身能够构成一个有价值的学术世界，只有感觉，直觉可以引导批评家对一件作品的认识与理解。

我在他俩谈话的时候，拍摄了一些照片，是旁边的几个欧洲女学生在阳光下十分裸露地喝咖啡和聊天的内容。有个女孩的背影非常漂亮，她构成了物理世界中的风景，也构成了一旁形而上学的基础——艺术家或者"疯人"就是这样联想的。这时我看到，德国人推着箱子离开了，我们握手告别。看上去，那离去的背影尽管受到强烈的阳光照耀，也仍然有一丝分别的感怀，当然，那样的感受很可能只是我自己的。

Sartre said "hell is other people," but this might well be amended to "dissipation is other people." If you are not careful, fatuous babble will deplete your energy and wisdom. If communication is impossible, then why should one go on striving to communicate? If dialogue is impossible, why go on having dialogue? Time keeps telling us the answer to the riddle: time itself is the answer. Thus Wu Shanzhuan finally came out and said, "Actually, as for the world (of art), to have understanding and communication between three to five people is enough. To put it precisely, we only care about angst and friendship among a small number of people." Zhang Peili expressed his distaste for use of concepts by intellectuals. He had little faith that words in themselves could comprise a valid domain of scholarly thought. Only perception and intuition can guide critics toward genuine knowledge and understanding of a work.

While the two of them were talking, I took a few photographs. The subject of my photos was a group of European coeds unabashedly exposed to the sunlight, drinking coffee and conversing. One girl had a highly attractive back, such that the physical setting resolved into a scene around her, while her back served as a springboard for metaphysical flights around the edges—these were associations entertained by an artist or perhaps "crazy man" just then. At that moment I saw the German engineer pushing his trunk on his way out. We shook hands and said goodbye. As I watched his receding shape under the brilliant sun, I thought I detected a trace of regret at parting. Of course, that perception may have been a trick of my own eye.

When Wang Guangyi, Huang Zhuan, Xiao Quan, and some others got to San Servolo, it was already 9:00 a.m. in the morning in China, May 29th, but in Italy it was the hour of resplendent sunset. Along with this group came Chang Chang of *Sanlian Life* magazine and He Duoling's student Yu Changhong. Another person who came with them was Shui Ge, although he was no longer needed to work on Wu Shanzhuan's installation. The sun at the horizon was a wonderful sight. Its orange rays symbolized

王广义、黄专、肖全等人到达 San Servolo 的时间是国内29日清晨1点过，却是这里28日下午灿烂的黄昏。同路的还有《三联生活》的苌苌和何多苓的学生喻传红，以及已经无须参与吴山专作品安装的水哥。快落入地平线的阳光非常好看，橘红色的调子构成了大家见面时的高兴的象征，尽管这样的象征往往短暂而忧郁。

晚餐的时间到了，更多的人仍然在食堂外吃饭。苌苌给我们（吴山专、张培力、黄专、我以及王广义）几个拍下了多少有些幽暗的黑白照片。晚上，黄专将广义、山专和培力组织到广义的房间，我的理解是为苌苌提供一次采访的机会。事实也是这样。尽管我谈到了展览的最初的想法，但是，我以为举办这个展览没有任何必然的原因。要不是一次偶然去苏州的机会，我是没有冲动的。不好意思，近年来我爱上了苏州园林，当上海当代艺术馆馆长 Samuel 提出希望我能够支持叶放在VIU做一个园林计划时，我原则地答应了。以后，为了让这个机会更加有内容，让青城山美术馆群有一次有趣的展览活动，我最后决定了让美术馆群

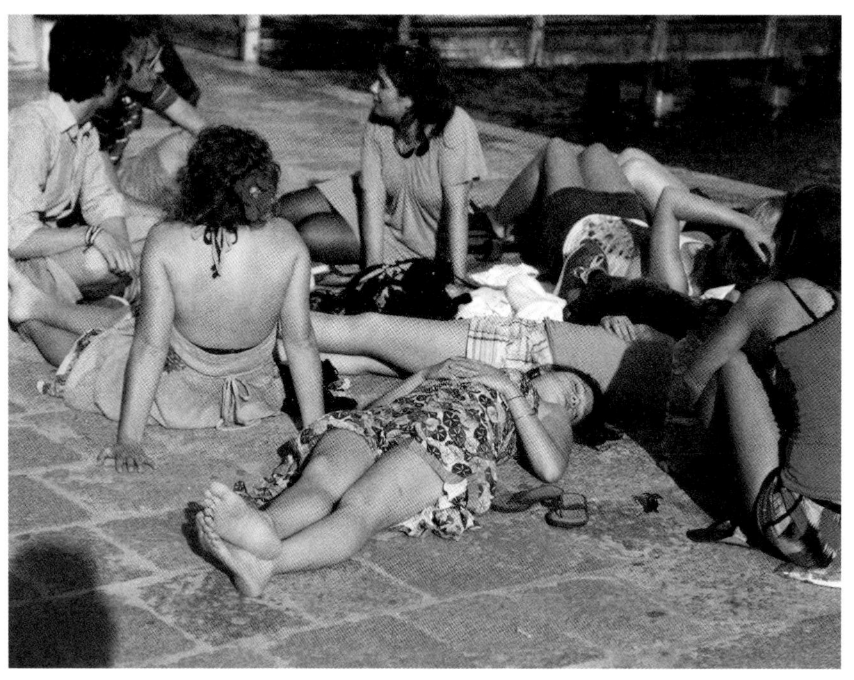

our happiness at seeing each other, though such symbolism is often fleeting and tinged with melancholy.

Time came for dinner, and more people opted to dine in the open air near the cafeteria. Chang Chang shot some rather shadowy photos of us (Wu Shanzhuan, Zhang Peili, Huang Zhuan, myself, and Wang Guangyi). That night Huang Zhuan invited Guangyi, Shanzhuan, and Peili to Guangyi's room. As I understood it, the aim was to give Chang Chang a chance to do interviews, and that is what she did. Although I talked about my original conception of the exhibition, I also maintained that there was no necessary reason for organizing it. If the chance for a trip to Suzhou had not come up, I would never have had this impulse. I must confess that in the past couple of years I have fallen in love with Suzhou. When Samuel Kung of the Shanghai Contemporary Museum asked if I could support Ye Fang's project on walled gardens at V.I.U., I approved in principle. Later, in order to add substance to the event, and to let Qingcheng Museum Complex be part of an interesting show, I finally decided to let our museum complex underwrite this exhibition. With support and much effort from V.I.U.'s president Umberto Vattani, in late February a collateral event of the Venice Biennial was born, which would feature the eight artists of the Qingcheng Museum Complex. As a matter of personal interest, and because of a long-planned Suzhou trip I had mentioned to Zhou Chunya several times, I decided that after my February trip to Venice was over I would invite everyone in our group to have some fun and discuss preparations for the show. So I arranged a gathering in Suzhou. In the past few years I have often gone to various walled gardens in the Jiangnan region. But this time it was April 9th and the sunlight was too strong. Wangshi Garden did not have the lush moistness I had experienced in the past. A walled garden needs rain, mist, and moisture to show its true temperament. In that early heat wave I had to look for a shady place to get away from the sun. I definitely wanted to hear some *kunqu* opera selections, even

承担了这次展览的经费。2月底，在VIU院长 Umberto Vattani（翁贝托·瓦塔尼）的支持与努力下，一个由青城山美术馆群八位艺术家为主导力量的第53届威尼斯国际艺术双年展特别邀请展 (a collateral event of 53th Biennnale di Venezia) 就诞生了。出于个人兴趣和与周春芽说过好几次要一块去苏州的计划，在决定参加威尼斯双年展之后，我想集中大家玩一下并利用机会跟大家商量展览的准备事宜，于是就在苏州安排了一次聚会。在最近的几年里，我经常去江南不同的园林。不过，4月9号那天苏州的阳光实在是太强烈了，网狮园没有了往日我体会到的润泽，园林需要雨、雾和潮湿，那是她的气质。所以，那天的园林不属于标准的园林，阳光灿烂，甚至有些过分的热，我还躲了一会阴凉地。的确，我本来也真的想听一听昆曲，尽管我完全不懂得她，也想让大家感受到传统的气质。这样的安排的确有些让人吃惊，何多说，如果不是我的这次安排，他可能永远不会到这里来。其实，我们在苏州雅集的另一个小任务，是共同完成一个册页，那是将送给VIU的礼物。

有很多人问过，为什么展览的题目叫"给马可波罗的礼物"？我想来想去，还是因为历史与园林提示了某种方向。马可波罗在他的《游记》里介绍过苏州与杭州。他使用了很美好的词汇去描述这两个城市的情况：

他到了华贵的城市"行在"（杭州），这个名字的含义就是"天堂之城"。这是一个非常卓越的描述，因为，毫无疑问，她是世界上最美和最华贵的城市。

八百多年前，马可波罗将中亚、西亚、东南亚等地区国家的山川地形，物产、气候、商贾贸易、居民、宗教信仰、风俗习惯，以及朝章国故、琐闻佚事告诉欧洲人，为欧洲人描绘出了难以置信的"神话"。马可波罗告诉威尼斯人，"地中海"不是世界的中心，新的世界地图需要重新绘制。在以后的东西方交流中，那些"神话"的书写者综合了人类不同文明。看来应该感谢马可波罗，就是这个简单的原因，我想，我们应该给他回敬一个礼物，去感谢他，呼应他。我们要去的城市是威尼斯，那不是马可波罗的故乡吗？没有任何一个要素不让我们接近 Marco Polo 这个符号和声音，有些离不开，躲不掉。我于2月9日在 San Servolo 11号楼的房间给艺术家们的第一份报告中这样写道：

展览的主题"给马可波罗的礼物"一目了然，她涉及到了东

though I do not understand them very well. I wanted our group to get a sense of traditional temperament. My arrangement was a surprise to some. He Duoling said if I had not arranged this, he might never have visited such a place. Our literati gathering in Suzhou had another purpose: we would create an album leaf jointly as a gift to V.I.U.

Many people asked me why we named the exhibition "A Gift to Marco Polo." I thought about it and realized that I had taken a cue from history and old walled gardens. Marco Polo in his *Travels* gave an account of Suzhou and Hangzhou, writing in rapturous terms about the beauties of those cities: *He reaches the splendid city of Kinsai, whose name means "City of Heaven." It well merits the description, because it is without doubt the finest and most splendid city in the world.*

Eight hundred years ago, Marco Polo told Europeans about the landforms, products, climate, commerce, customs, and modes of rule of Central and East Asian countries, describing what had once been only a myth. Marco Polo told the Venetians that the "Mediterranean" was not the middle of the world, and a new map of the world would have to be drawn. In the subsequent exchanges between East and West, inscribers of myth forged a synthesis out of different civilizations. Clearly we owe thanks to Marco Polo for this simple reason. I felt that we should respond to him and thank him with a gift. Soon we would be going to Venice—was that not his native place? There was nothing to keep us from availing ourselves of a symbol and voice like Marco Polo. In a way it was a topic we could not get away from. On February 9th, from my room in Building 11 on San Servolo, I wrote my first report to the artists:

As an exhibition theme, "A Gift to Marco Polo" is quite straightforward. It touches on the East and West, on history and today, on civilization and tradition, and on the stance and attitude of contemporary art in the course of globalization. So this show will be a good chance for experimentation. Considering that the setting is rich with temporal layering,

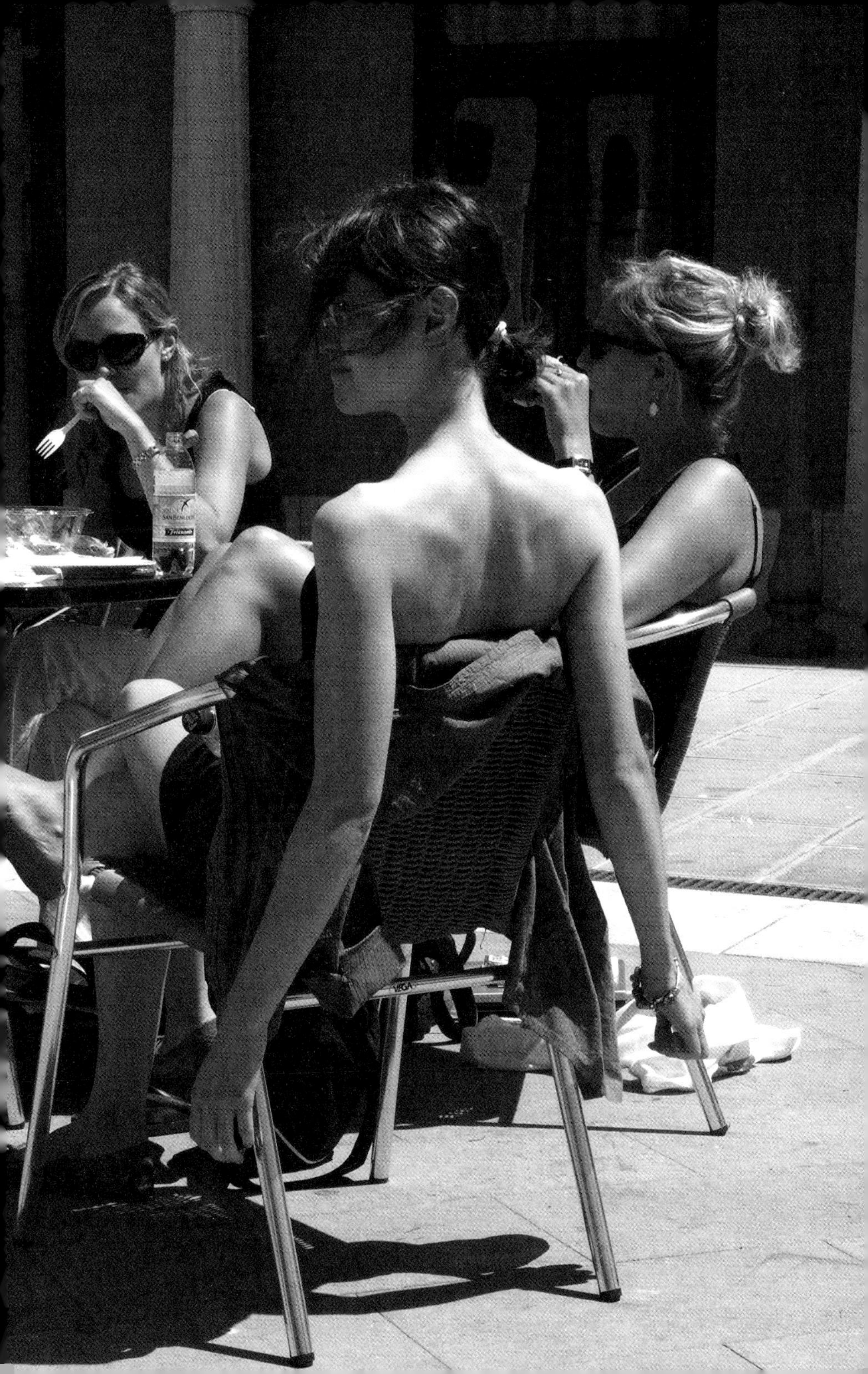

this will also be an occasion for heightened interfusion with the surroundings.

My description sounded a bit hollow, but obviously I felt something infectious at San Servolo. I hoped very much that my associates could come and cavort there. After breathing the turbid air back in China, it would be wonderful to spend time in a place of gulls' cries and boat whistles! I realized that in both mind and body I had been longing for a more suitable setting.

Wang Guangyi was the second person to speak at length. In half-veiled terms he admitted why he was using the Old Summer Palace for subject matter. He said it was definitely not to deliver a judgment about history; rather, it was to provide a setting in which multiple interpretations were possible. From the time that Marco Polo had set foot on Chinese soil, the relation of China and Italy had worked out in convoluted ways. He said that the Old Summer Palace, as "physical evidence" of history, was a salient reminder of cultural and political clashes. At the same time, the Old Summer Palace was a "crime scene" for the Eight Allied Armies' act of invading and plundering China. Of course this was unforeseeable not only to Marco Polo but also to Giuseppe Castiglione, who had helped design the Old Summer Palace. He wanted to restore an "on-site feel" to history, and to let Marco Polo's descendants know the complexity of this segment of history. I felt that sad reflection upon dark chapters of history and a sorrowful sense of temporality can become, on an occasion like this, a matter for today. To be sure, Guangyi had his own stance: a strong sense of nationality, perhaps even nationalism, ran in his blood, which is why he brought up the idea of "invasion." An American I met told me that the word "invasion" should not be applied casually to eras prior to establishment of modern society, when national boundaries were not clearly drawn up. Look at your own Genghis Khan and think of how one should categorize his three westward campaigns. Of course, this is not a simple question. At any rate I caught Guangyi's implied meaning: he was not happy with Western attitudes toward China.

方与西方，历史与今天，文明与传统，以及关于全球化进程中当代艺术的立场与态度，所以，这次展览是一次很好的实验机会。鉴于展览的场所与环境具有优雅的时间色彩，所以，展览将同时也是一次与环境的高度融合。

这些描述有些空洞，但是，我显然受到了 San Servolo 环境的感染。我很希望大家到这里来玩一玩。国内的空气很肮脏，有海鸥叫和汽笛声的地方难道不是一个好的去处！这个时候，我发现自己的身心在寻找一个更加适合它的环境。

王广义是第二个主要说话的人，他含含糊糊地交代了为什么要使用圆明园这个历史的素材。他说他根本不是为了对历史做出什么评价，不过是提供一个有可能得到多重解释的现场。从马可波罗踏上中国的土地之后，"意大利与中国在漫长的历史长河中构成了极其复杂的关系"。他说，"圆明园作为历史的'物证'，具有特别的意义。包含了复杂的文化与政治的冲突。同时圆明园又是八国联军对中国的军事侵略与文化掠夺的'犯罪现场'。当然，不仅马可波罗，就是圆明园的设计者之一朗世宁 (F. Giuseppe Castiglione) 也不会想到这一点。"他希望还原历史的"现场"，让马可波罗的后人理解到历史与文化的复杂性。我想，在这个现场里，对历史的感伤，对灾难的反省以及对充满悲剧的时间的缅怀，都成为今天的问题。其实，广义仍然有自己的立场，他的身体里流淌着一种民族甚至种族主义的血液，所以，他使用了"侵略"这个概念。一个美国人告诉我，在人类的现代社会还没有建立起来，国家疆界并不明确的时期，"侵略"这个词不要随便使用，你看看你们的成吉思汗 (Genghis Khan)，三次西征应该算什么呢？这当然不是一个简单的问题，不过，我读得出广义的含义。他不高兴西方人对中国的态度，他几乎是本能地具有一种文明冲突不可避免的心理状态。

培力对回答记者的问题有些发蹙。培力是一个不喜欢命题作文的艺术家，他从来是从自己的某种感受出发，就像他在头一天与老吴谈到的那样，感觉与知觉的复杂性导致了一件作品的出发点的产生。很多年前，他为一只鸡洗澡，直至这个生命濒临垂危；他摔下玻璃，再将破裂的玻璃用胶水粘连上，进而再次将玻璃摔碎，不断往复。你去问问他为什么在1988年之后要制作那些被夹有医用实物的玻璃作品，问问为什么要画出那些没有任何情绪的手套？在更早，我们知道培力画过有"萨克斯"的人物，那多少是他哥哥的爱好的被转换含义的记录。没有太多反映论的概

Almost instinctively he held a conviction that cultural conflict was inevitable.

Peili was a bit vexed with the reporter's question. Peili is an artist who does not like to create commissioned works. He always acts from what he perceives. As he told Wu Shanzhuan the first day, complexity of sensation and intuition were the point of departure for a work's creation. Several years before he had bathed a chicken until it was within an inch of its life. He had dropped a pane of glass, then painstakingly glued the broken pieces together, then repeated the process. He was sometimes asked why, after 1988, he created those glass pieces incorporating medical accessories, or why he painted expressionless surgical gloves. He was also asked why he painted those figures holding saxophones, which was perhaps an allusion to his brother's hobby. But concepts of mirroring reality never went far toward explaining Peili's works. At times he made statements about art, but his essay "The Battle of Art" seemed to have no direct connection with his own works. This time, likewise, Peili hoped to avoid an explanatory message. But no one would doubt that his work *Tower*, done for this show, was a symbol of copying and interchange between cultures. I think it was Guangyi who chimed in after Peili, saying that interchange between civilizations was no more than a process of falling under the sway of alternating "strongholds." Even the Old Summer Palace designed by Castiglione was no more than European architecture rendered in a stronghold-like mode. Were not the great classic works of architecture merely "strongholds" designed to serve as models? I think he raised an interesting question.

Wu Shanzhuan spoke of Plato's story about "second-hand water." What implication can be ascribed to water that comes from the hands of a woman whom one passes beside a riverbank? His question was of course an intellectual formulation, a relatively sealed-off game of words. Wu's notions have always had this truncated quality, and he has never set out to link them up. But what kind of "rigorous issues" can fragmentary symbols provide?

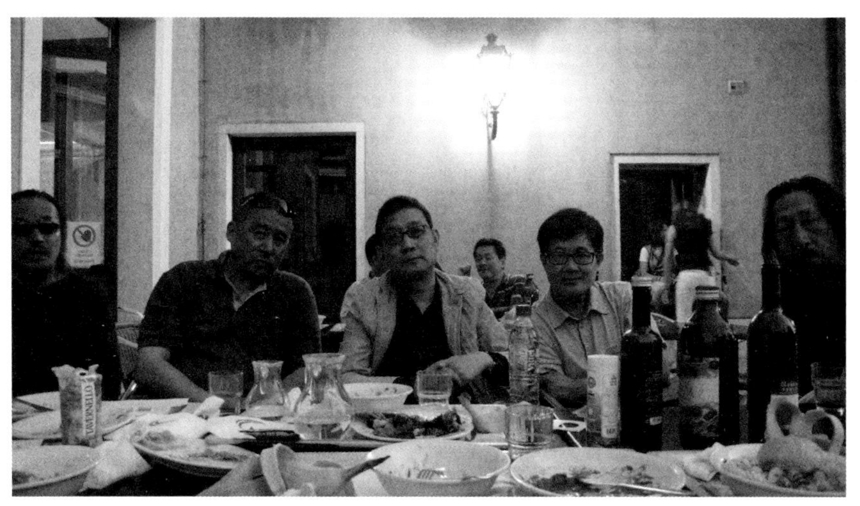

念能够解释培力的作品，他自己也有关于自己的艺术的陈述，但是，他的文章"为艺术而战"似乎也与自己的作品没有直接的关系。这次，培力同样希望避免说明性的含义，可是，谁也不会怀疑，他提供的"塔"成为文明之间相互拷贝与交流的象征。好像是广义接着培力的话，人类文明之间的交流不过是互为"山寨"的过程，就是朗世宁设计的圆明园，也不过是一个山寨版的欧洲建筑。真正的经典又何尝不是一种作为范本的"山寨"呢？这是一个有趣的问题。

吴山专讲到了柏拉图的"二手水"的故事，通过路过河边一位妇女转手得到的水，将有可能具有什么新的含义？这当然是智慧的编造，是一种语词的相对封闭的游戏。吴的念头是断裂的，从来就没有连起来过，可是，散碎的符号能够给我们提供什么样的"硬问题"？就像黄专几天前在"梧桐"说的那样，我们不能被简单的社会学逻辑和道德主义责任给干扰，人类艺术完成的仅仅是观念递进的任务。然而，什么观念被认为属于人类的遗产并成为观念史中的一环呢？语词再次构成了阻力，除非我们的权力为某个观念提供了合法性的支撑，而这样的问题刚好不属于观念讨论的范围，所以，如何能够提供一个共识性的结论仍然变得非常困难，这也是为什么吴的作品总是受到一些批评家的质疑的原因——一个艺术家的观念在什么条件下能够成为有价值的东西？这个问题是难以回答的。

Just as Huang Zhuan had said a few days before at "Scholartree," we cannot let sociological logic or moralistic duty interfere with us. What art accomplishes for human beings is simply the mission of advancing ideas. But what ideas are considered a human legacy and will be taken up into the history of ideas? Here once again words will comprise an obstacle unless our power can provide support for an idea's legitimacy. Yet such an issue falls outside the scope addressed by ideas. The question of how to put forth a consensual conclusion still presents difficulty. This is the reason that Wu's creations are often questioned by critics. Under what conditions does an artist's idea become something of value? This question is hard to answer.

Partway through the discussion Huang Zhuan said he was tired and went back to his room to sleep. We did not hear his point of view. Before long, physical exhaustion chased us all back to our rooms. Once again, metaphysics yielded to the laws of the physical world, and we laid down to rest.

　　黄专说他疲倦了，讨论中途就回到他的房间睡觉去了。我们没有听到他的意见。很快，来自生理上的困顿将我们所有的人赶回房间，形而上学再次接受了物理世界的法则，我们都躺下了。

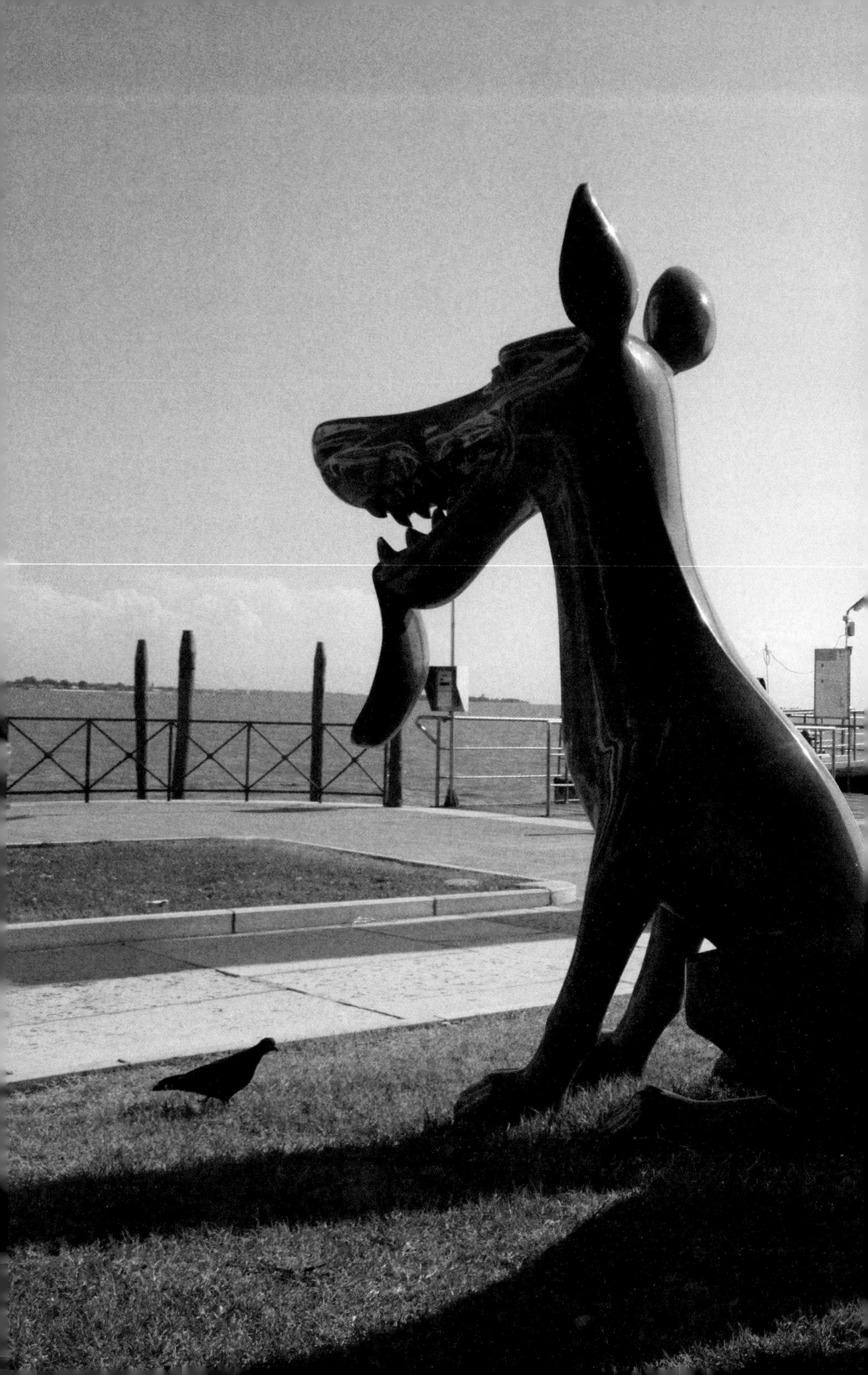

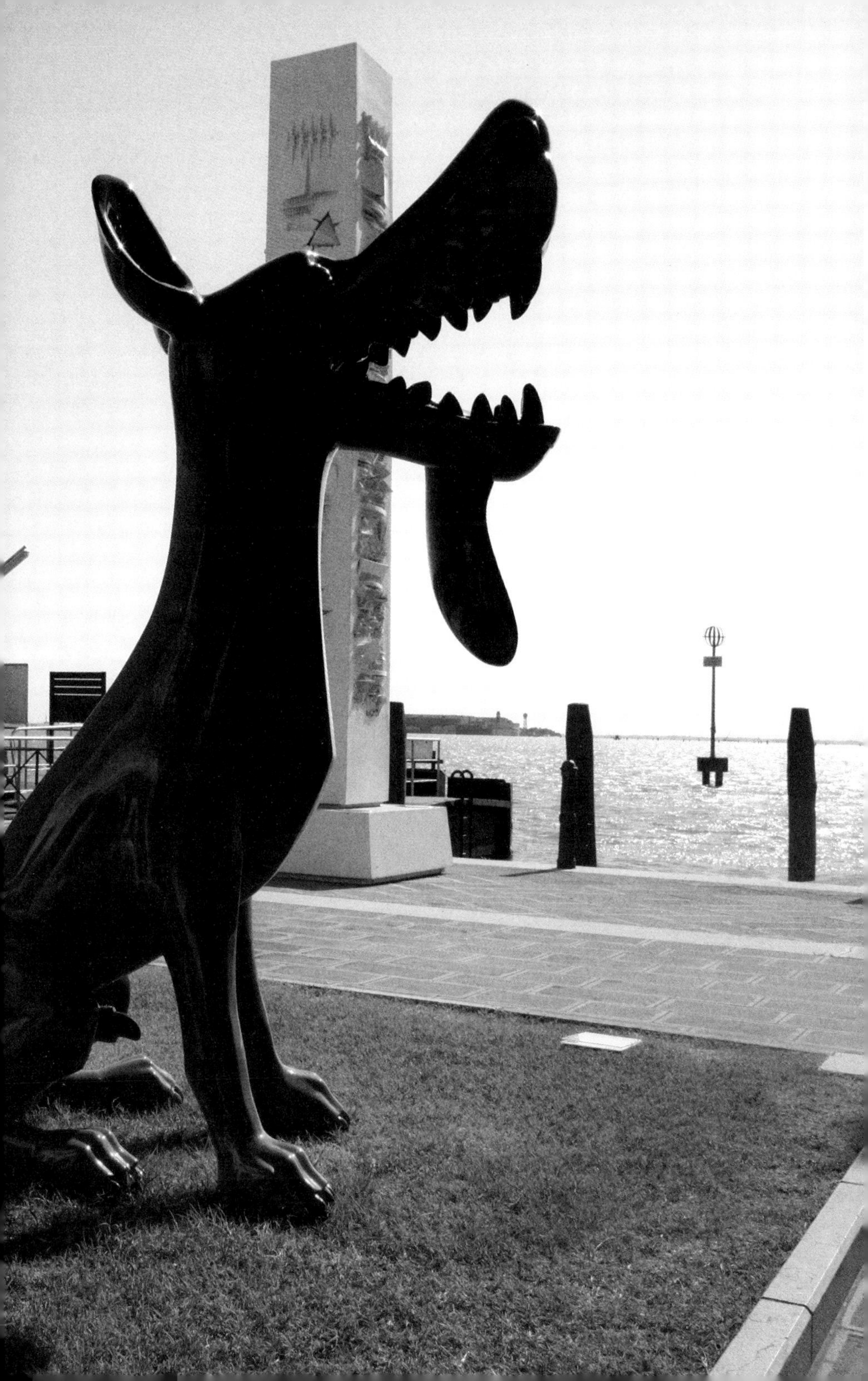

May 29th

On the 29th Guangyi went to the site to complete his creation, and Xiao Quan went along to photograph the whole process. Guangyi had twelve of Castiglione's design drawings for the Old Summer Palace sandwiched between clear acrylic panels and set atop ten tons of architectural rubble. This hinted that we were at the Old Summer Palace's site of destruction by the Eight Allied Armies, even though Guangyi continually told us that his intent was not tendentious, but only a way of offering a range of associations. Early in the morning Xiao Quan photographed us in the soft sunlight as we strolled along the shore of San Servolo reveling in the pristine air. I remembered when I went to Wuhan with Xiao Quan in 1991 and met with some of the artists there: Wang Guangyi, Shu Qun, Ren Jin, Wei Guangqing. We talked about possibilities for new art in the aftermath of 1989. From 1990 to 1992 I went to Wuhan several times, and one time I saw Zhang Peili. That was the period when Derrida's ideas were popular, and people often used expressions like "the abyss of substance" and "bottomless chessboard." Indeed, at a time when Southwest artists still felt acute unease over the severe political reality, artists in Wuhan seemed to have put aside real-world problems brought on by events in Tiananmen Square two years before. Starting in 1991 the idea of a commodity economy was gradually replaced by the "market economy," and by 1992 people were no longer confined by older ideas. So one could often hear Wuhan artists use the phrase "transformative extension." At the time it made me think of terms like "coherency" and "ideal pattern" that had become

<h1 style="text-align:center">5月29日</h1>

29日是广义去现场完成他的作品的时间。肖全跟着他拍摄了整个过程。广义将他夹有朗世宁圆明园设计图的十二块有机玻璃板安放在十吨建筑废灰上面，他暗示这个地方就是八国联军当时毁掉的圆明园现场，尽管他不断告知他不打算带有任何倾向，而仅仅是给观众提供思考与联想的可能性。这天清晨，肖全给我们拍摄了一些照片，清晨的阳光柔和之至，我们围着 San Servolo 岛边缓缓散步，领略空气的清新。记得在1991年的时候，我和肖全到武汉，与在那里的王广义、舒群、任戬、魏光庆见面。我们讨论1989年之后新艺术的可能性。从1990年到1992年，我去了好几

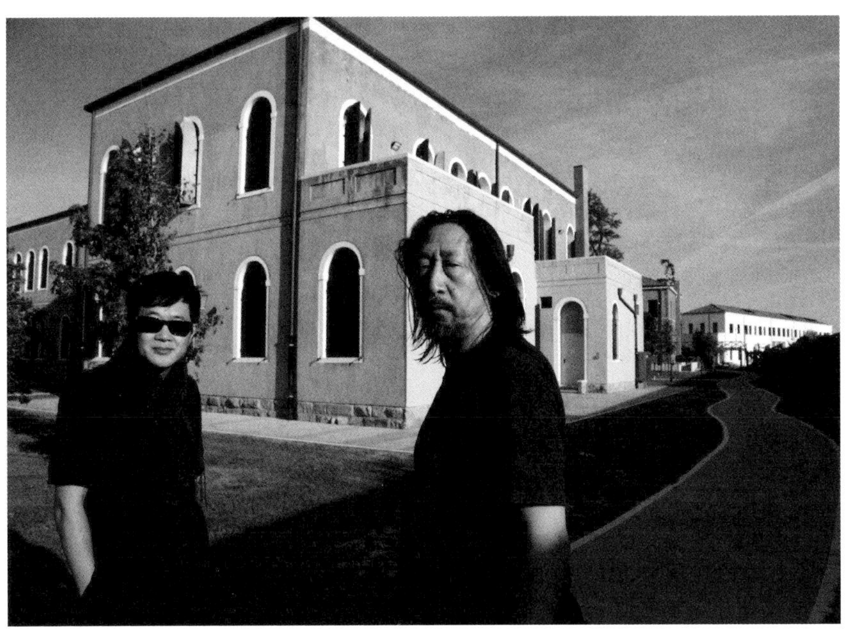

current among artists' groups in the north a few years before. I did not know how the use of these neologisms was fostered, but I found the atmosphere to be contagious. One day Huang Zhuan awaited me in his little room. I was told that the Wuhan artists had arranged this get-together, hoping to hear us debate on scholarly issues. They said that Huang Zhuan followed the methodology of Ernst Gombrich, with Fan Jingzhong as his backup. (Later Fan Jingzhong became my doctoral advisor.) Later I put Yan Shanchun of the Wuhan Art Institute in touch with Shao Hong and Yang Xiaoyan in Guangzhou. I felt that they had things in common, and I could not equal their knowledge. By 1992 I had gone to dinner at Huang Zhuan's flat in the Guangzhou Art Institute dormitory. At this point, some people had already moved to the South. My memories of Wuhan are many sided. The photos that Xiao Quan took of me with Wang Guangyi at Sanhan Gong accurately document our spiritual outlook and mode of being at the time: independent, youthful, retaining our ideals, ready to issue forth to make our mark, but in many respects having only limited resources. Around this time Guangyi formulated his all-out critique. When the familiar iconic images (worker, peasant, soldier) began appearing on canvases in his studio, I was aware that new art was making an appearance. Whether in handling abstract patterns or representative figures, Wang Guangyi consistently concerned himself with what were termed conceptual issues. He looked for images that people were familiar with, but he said they bore little relation to their original historical background. He said that he had broken open the original logic of his images in order to make them become blind spots. People saw him present works with Mao Zedong superimposed on a grid, and heard him say he was "clearing up humanistic enthusiasm," and saw him invoke the idea of "all-out critique," but he claimed these things did not have any relation to the reality of "workers, peasants, and soldiers." Now he was putting Castiglione's design drawings on exhibit, as if to tell the Italians: "Look, the Old Summer Palace was the creation of an Italian, but now it has been reduced to rubble."

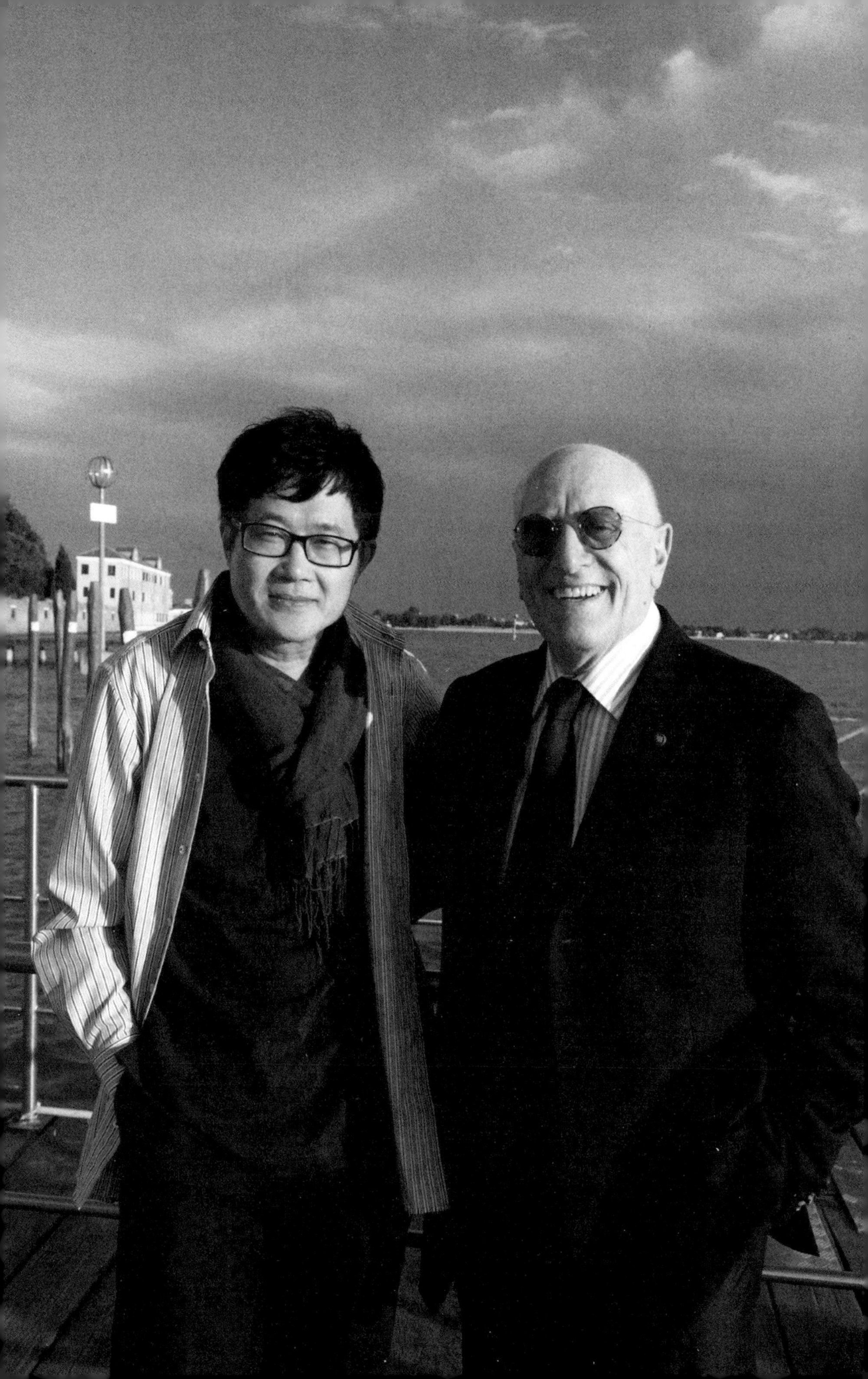

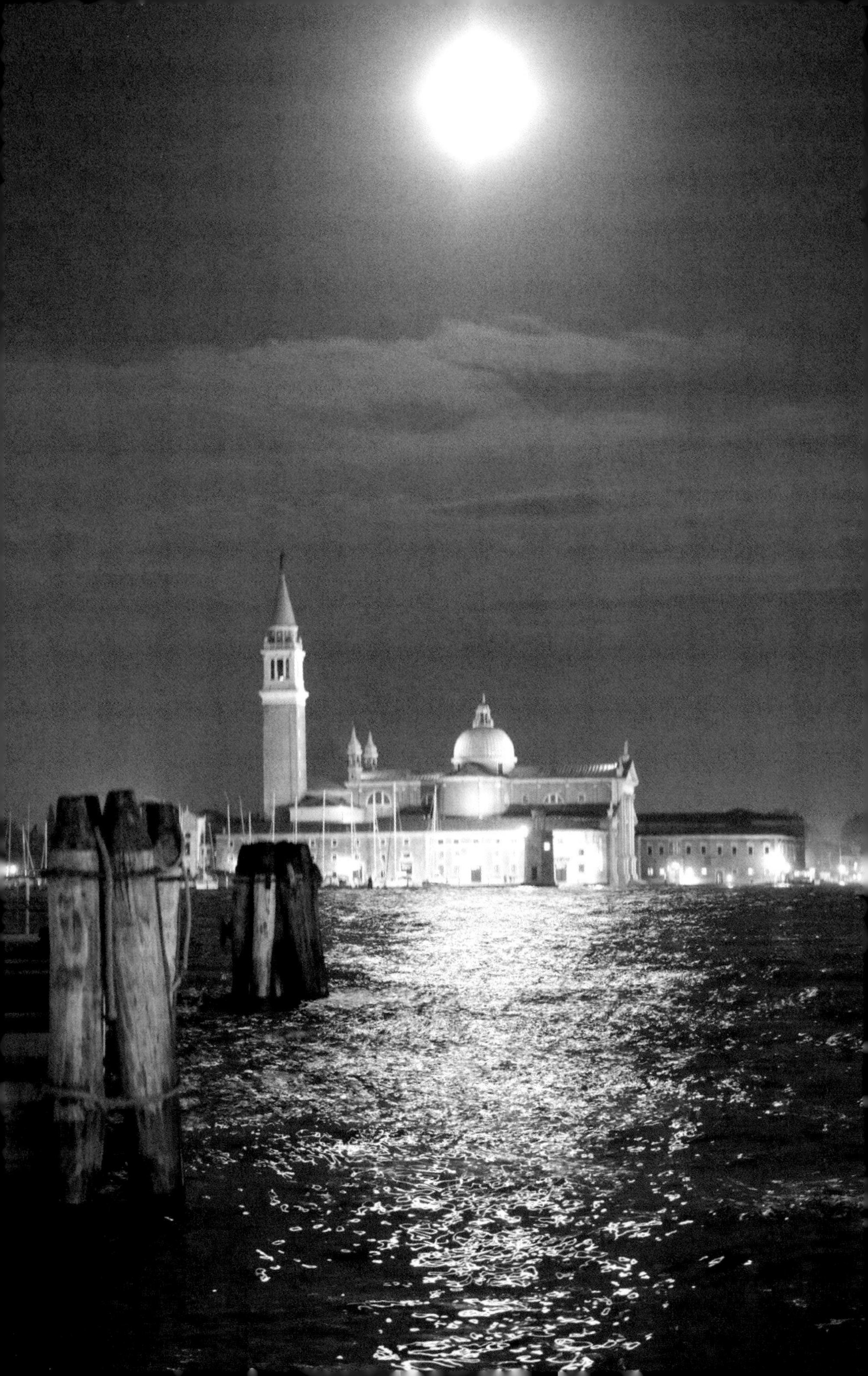

次武汉，有一次还见到了培力。这正是德里达 (Jacques Derrida) 的概念流行的时候，大家经常有"本质的深渊"、"无底的棋盘"这样的表述。的确，当西南艺术家还在为严峻的政治与现实感到极度的不安时，在武汉的艺术家似乎已经将两年前天安门广场引发的现实问题放在了一边。的确，商品经济的概念在1991年之后开始逐渐为"市场经济"所替代，直到1992年，人们不再囿于旧有的概念。所以，在武汉艺术家的嘴里，你可以经常听到"延异"这个词，那时，我联想到的是好几年前北方艺术家群体对"理式"或者"理念"这类词汇的借用。我还不清楚这个习惯是怎样培养出来的，我被武汉的空气所感染。一天，黄专在他的小屋里等着我们，据说，是艺术家们挑起来，希望看到我与黄专辩论学术问题，他们说黄专是贡布里希 (Ernst Hans Gombrich) 方法论这个路子的，有范景中（范景中后来是我的博士生导师，我也成为了他的学生）作为后盾。那以后，我把在武汉美术院的严善錞，和在广州的邵宏、杨小彦联系起来，我觉得他们都是一帮人，我的知识不如他们。很快，1992年，我已经在广州美术学院的宿舍黄专的家里吃饭了，这时，湖北的人都迁徙到了南方。对武汉的记忆来自很多方面，肖全给我和广义在三涵宫拍摄的照片成为那时我们的精神面貌和现实的准确记录：独立、年轻、仍然保持着理想、准备再次出击、但是所拥有的资源仍然有限。广义的大批判就是在这个时候产生的。当我们熟悉的形象（工人、农民与解放军）出现在他的画室里的画布上时，我意识到新艺术已经开始。从抽象的概念到具体的形象，王广义始终关注的是一些被称之为"观念"的问题，他寻找人们熟悉的形象，却说这个形象与其本身的历史背景没有关系，他说他拆开了形象原有的逻辑，不过是让作品提供盲点。人们在他提供了打格子的毛泽东的作品的同时，听到他说他要"清理人文热情"；见到了他的"大批判"，他却不认为那些"工农兵"与现实有什么关系。现在，他将朗世宁的设计图放在那里，告诉意大利人：这圆明园可是意大利人的作品，然而今天已经成为废墟。广义没有说他想指责意大利人，可是，他知道八国联军有意大利的军队。张培力说，有资料表明烧毁圆明园的是英法联军，可是我们也知道，历史文献也表明，在前前后后的破坏中，同样有关于意大利军队参与的记录。广义的作品从来就是这样，他提供人们熟悉的资源，却否认这个资源在自己作品中与原有逻辑的关系。事实上，他想打开任

Guangyi did not say that he wanted to rebuke the Italians, but he knew the Eight Allied Armies included Italian troops. Zhang Peili said there were sources indicating that the Old Summer Palace was destroyed by the English and French allied armies. Yet we also know there are documents showing that the Italian troops, at some points, also participated in the destruction. Guangyi's pieces are always like this: he provides resources with which people are familiar, but denies that the iconic elements in his pieces have anything to do with their original logic. In fact, he wants to open them to any possibility. Apparently he wants to affirm that the charisma of art lies in the unlimited derivation of possibilities.

That afternoon all the artists' creations were in place at the exhibition space. Umberto Vattani was quite moved as he shared his feelings about their works with me. In his office he gave his analysis of each piece, showing an in-depth understanding of Yue Minjun's work especially. While speaking of Yue's pieces, he trenchantly contrasted elements of imagery used in Eastern and Western cultures. That day Umberto Vattani invited me to dinner at a seaside restaurant on Lido Island, where we had a twilight view of San Servolo in the distance. As the setting sun neared the horizon, San Servolo gradually turned to a silhouette. Umberto Vattani said that it was quite a pretty view. I was used to statements like this in everyday life and had to concur that the view was indeed pretty. What Umberto Vattani said next left an impression on me: nature is marvelous. Every quarter hour it is liable to change. In fact the scenes we see do not repeat themselves. Thus we can see countless beautiful pictures, each different, in the same place. I gained insight from his description: I have been too inattentive to variations that happen every day. Indeed, in just a few minutes we can witness plentiful changes in the coloring of the sky and the ocean's surface. The miraculous alterations of a scene give us a sense that one setting changes to another. After nine o'clock the sun quickly sank beneath the horizon. The orange world turned into a ruddy red one, and then night finally fell.

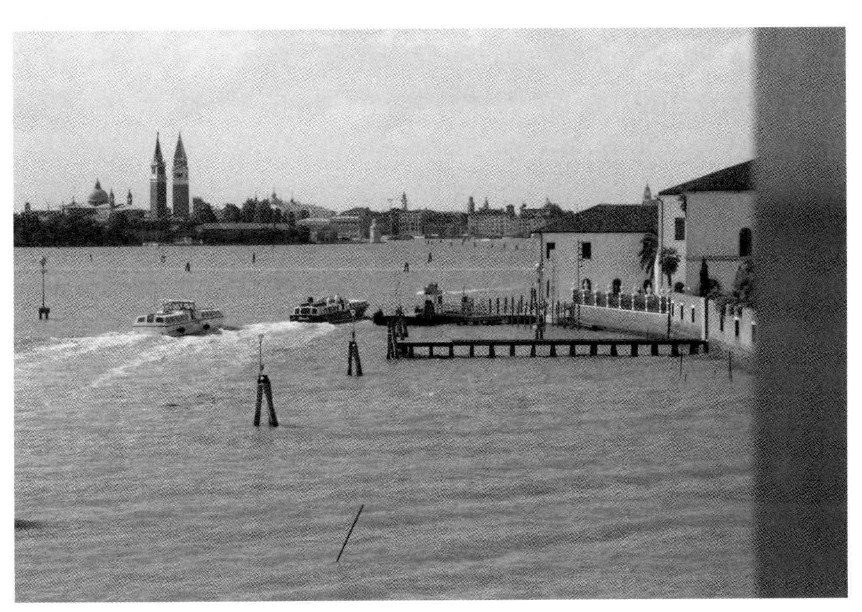

何可能性，他似乎确认，艺术的魅力就存在于可能性的无限衍生。

这天下午，艺术家们的作品都已经在展览空间呈现，Umberto Vattani 很激动地与我交换了他对艺术家们的作品的感想，在办公室，他对展览作品一一进行了分析，他尤其表达了对岳敏君作品的充分理解，他在说到岳的作品时，把东西方文明的形式因素进行了很细腻的对比。当天，Umberto Vattani 请我到 LiDo 岛上的一个靠海的餐厅共进晚餐。黄昏里，从我们的餐馆可以眺望不远处的 San Servolo，当落日接近地平线的时候，San Servolo 渐渐变成了一个剪影。Umberto Vattani 说，这里看上去的风景非常漂亮。日常生活中，我熟悉这样的描述，显然，这里的风景看上去非常漂亮。但是，给我印象深刻的是，Umberto Vattani 说：自然是奇妙的，每一刻都会有变化，我们看到的风景其实是不会重复的，这样，我们在同样一个地方就能看到无数不同的美丽图画。这样的描述让我获得了启迪，我对日常的变化实在是太不注意，也太粗糙了，的确，几分种的时间，我们已经目睹了天空与海面上色彩的丰富变化，风景本身奇迹般的改变让我们感到如同更换环境一般。晚上九点之后，太阳迅速落下地平线，金黄色的世界变成了暗红色……黑夜终于降临。

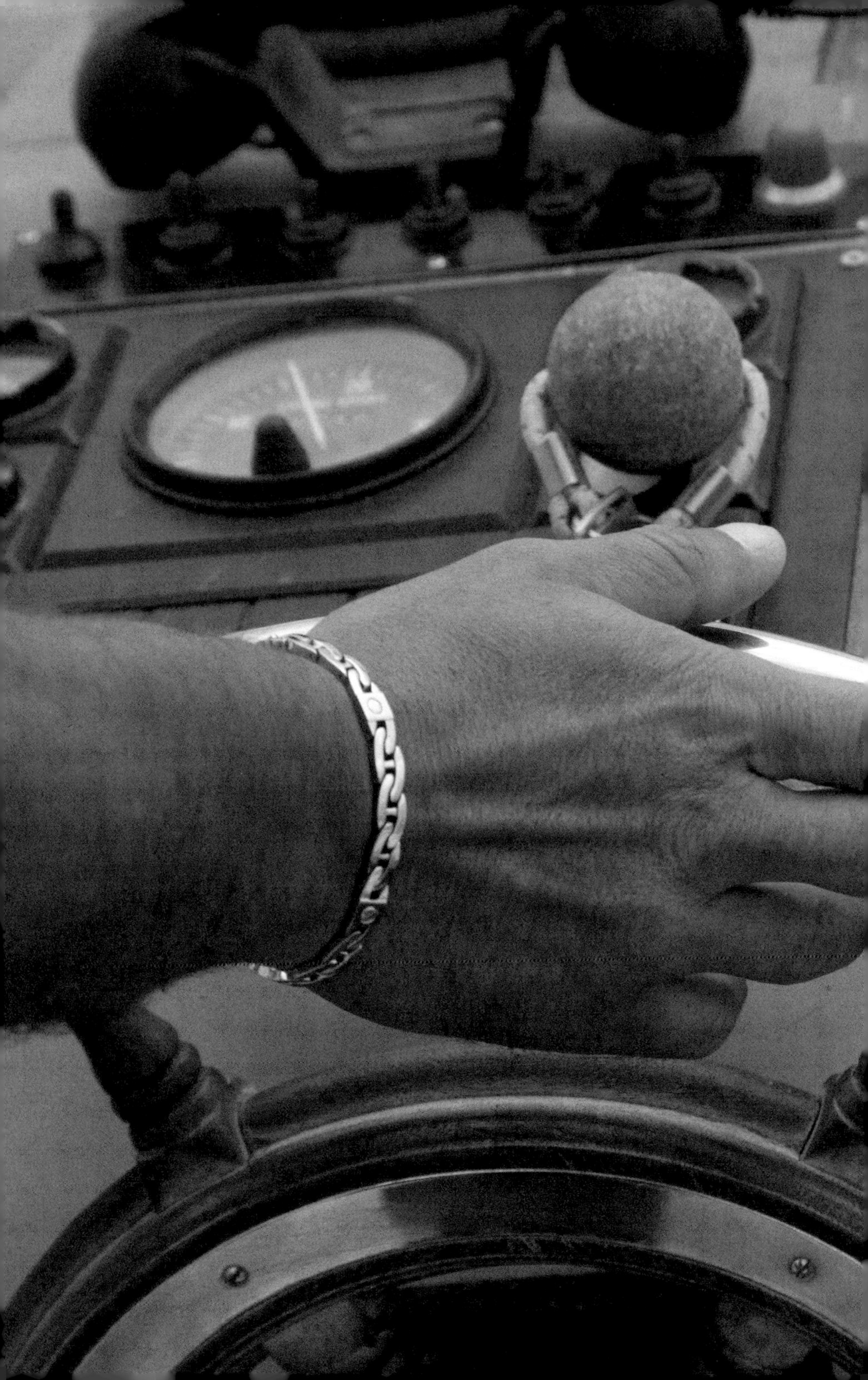

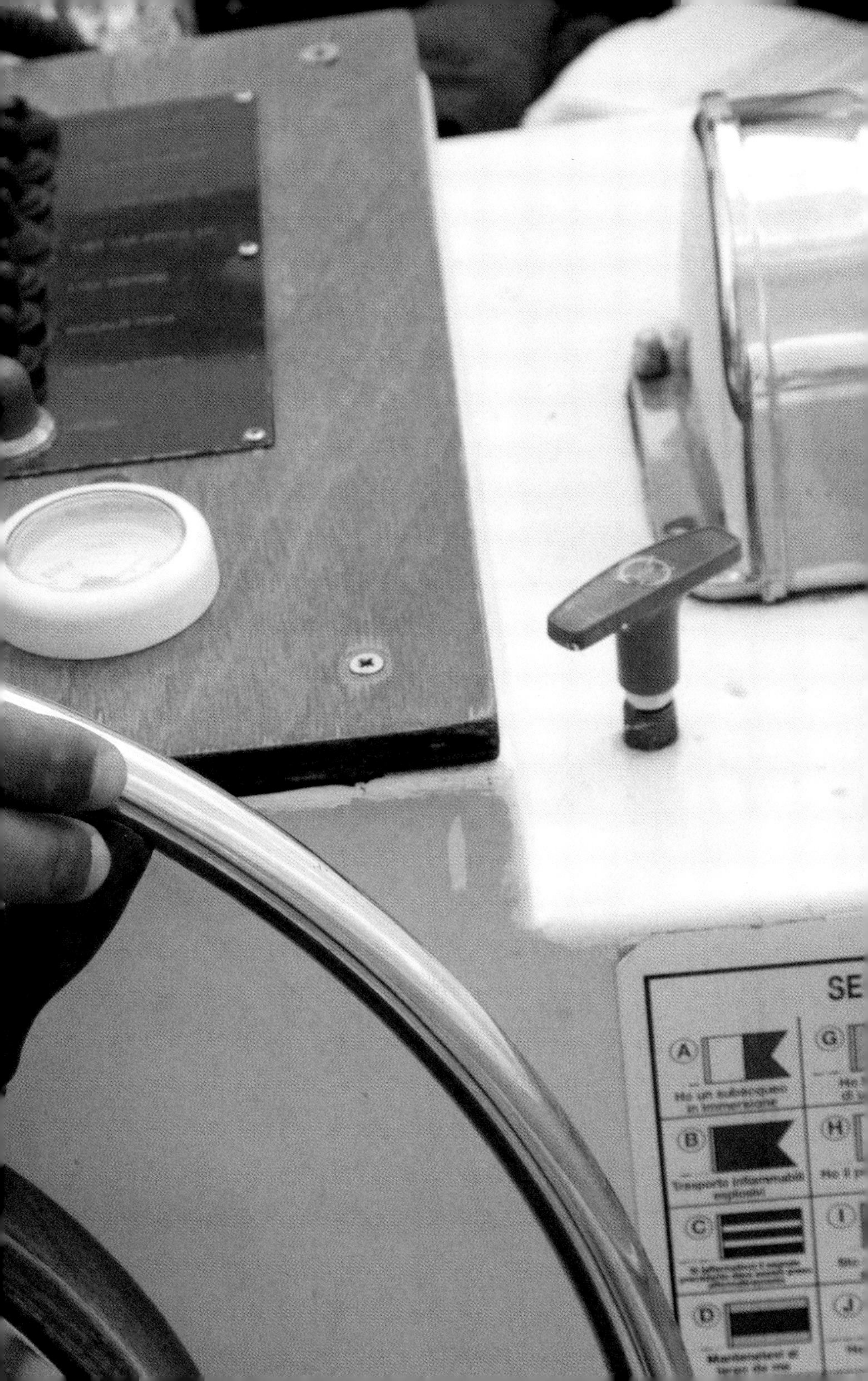

SE
A No un subacqueo in immersione
G
B Trasporto infiammabili esplosivi
H
C
I
D Mantenment al largo de me
J

May 30th

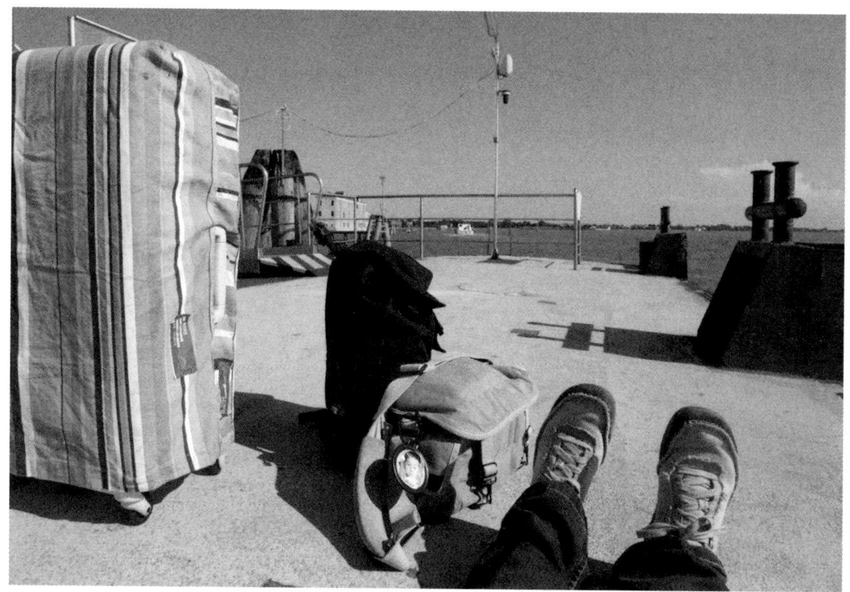

On the 30th our poster designer and his two assistants had to deal with tasks involving on-site advertising and guide markers on the main island. After four hectic days on San Servolo, we finally had the leisure to visit the main island. Yu Chuanhong, a student of He Duoling whom we had met at the gathering in Suzhou, planned to meet a friend who was in Venice, so we all went to the main island together. I met with Xiao Quan, Yin Jiulong, and his assistant on Piazza San Marco.

At the suggestion of Yin Jiulong, we made an excursion to see the aquatic sights of Venice in a gondola. We sat outside at Piazza

5月30日

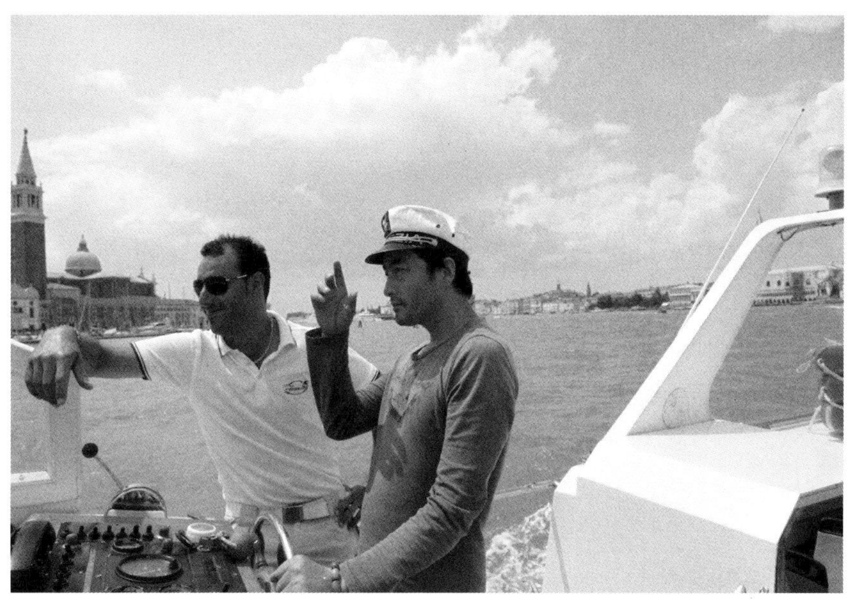

30日，一些涉及现场包装指示系统的工作需要平面设计师殷九龙和他的助手去本岛解决。在 San Servolo 已经紧张了四天，终于，有空闲去本岛了。在苏州雅集认识的何多的学生喻传红本来要与她在威尼斯的朋友见面，这样，我们一块到了本岛，在圣马可广场的红色咖啡区域与肖全、殷九龙以及他的助手见了面。

在殷九龙等人的建议下，我们乘坐 Gondola 在威尼斯水城中游荡。我们一行在圣马可广场的露天倾听音乐，任何到过威尼斯的人会同意，这是美好的地方，尽管音乐很重复，在这里，我更愿意说：美的就是美的，很多听过的音乐仍然会让人内心荡漾。听觉会保持记忆，广场各个咖啡厅外面表演的很多音乐让人

San Marco listening to music. Anyone who passes through Venice will admit that this is a beautiful spot. Even though the music tended to repeat itself, I have to admit that its beauty was not diminished. Many musical pieces that one has heard before can still stir a person's heart. The auditory sense preserves memory: much of the music performed at cafes along the Piazza made me recall scenes from my life in the 1980s. I used to listen to Western classical music on low-fidelity tapes re-recorded from the collection of one friend or another (in Chengdu these included Yi Dan, Zhou Chunya, and Zhang Xiaogang). Of course the selection included Russian music by composers like Rachmaninoff. The low quality did not detract from our enjoyment and understanding of Western music. On this occasion, those graceful melodies were part of the setting provided to consumers at a scenic attraction. The casual air of sightseers strolling by undermined the sense of sacredness we had once felt inwardly toward Western music.

This was the first day I was not loaded down with work. Once back on San Servolo, I saw that aside from some adjustments still necessary for Zhang Peili's *Tower*, the exhibition's set-up had been completed.

回想到80年代的情境，我经常用十分拙劣的磁带录音机听着从这个人那个人（在成都经常是易丹、周春芽、张晓刚）那里转录过来的西方古典音乐（当然也包括像拉赫玛尼诺夫这样的俄罗斯作品），可是，那完全没有影响我们对西方音乐的欣赏与理解，今天，那些悠扬的旋律不过是旅游胜地里的一个消费内容，广场来往的游人所构成的轻松气氛减弱了我们当年内心对西方音乐的神圣性的对待。

这天是我唯一没有太多工作的一天，回到 San Servolo，我们看到，除了张培力需要对他的"塔"进行更精细的调试，展览布置已经全部结束。

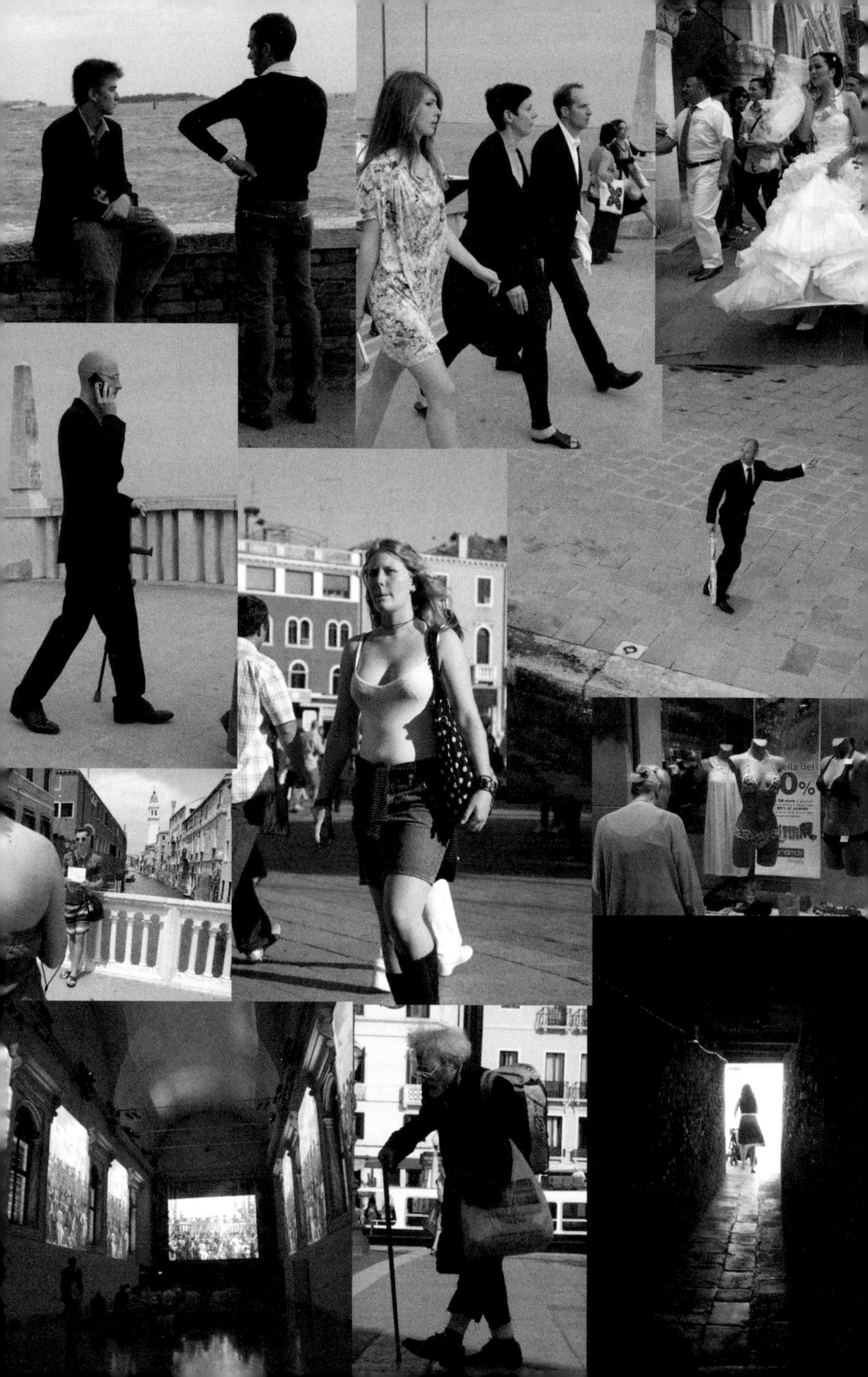

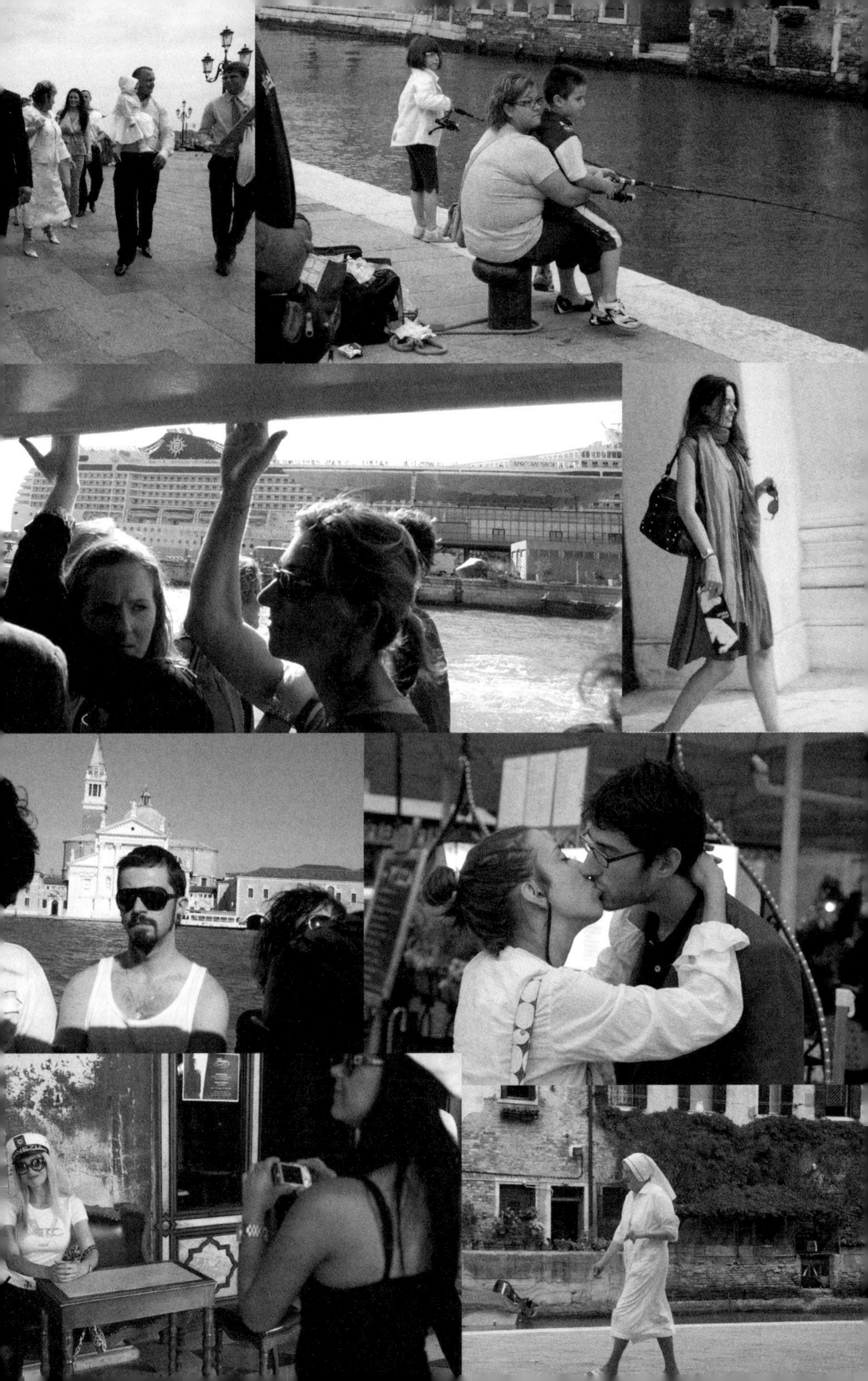

June 1st

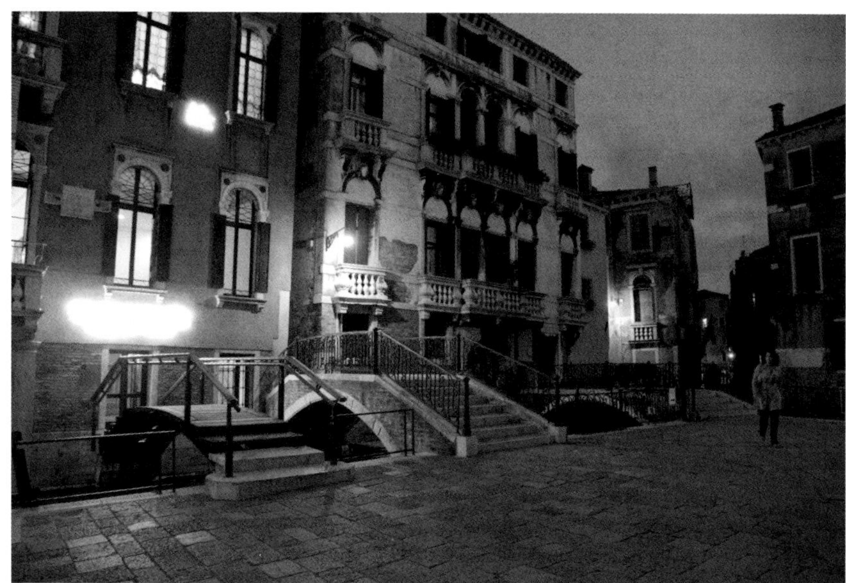

On June 1st at 11 a.m. Italian time, the last contingent of our group arrived at San Servolo by water taxi. The two boats pulled up side by side at the dock, and the awaited faces appeared one by one from the boats' cabins: Yue Minjun, Zhang Xiaogang, He Duoling, Zhou Chunya… One by one they came onto the bank: Gao Shiming, Liu Chun, Leng Lin, Zhu Zhu. There was a long list of people: He Duoling's girl friend Zheng Yue and Li Sa who had come over from the main island to see her, as well as Nie Rongqing, Shuang Shuang, Bruce Doar, and Sun Yue.

It was a day of glorious weather, and any common camera

6月1日

意大利6月1日上午不到11点的时间，最后的大队伍乘 water taxi 到达了 San Servolo，两条船并行在码头边，人头一个个地从船舱里伸出来：岳敏君、张晓刚、何多苓、周春芽……他们一个个地上岸，高士明、刘淳、冷林、朱朱，一串人的名单：何多的女朋友郑越、从本岛过来见何多的李飒、聂荣庆、霜霜、BRUCE、孙越。这是一个阳光灿烂的天气，任何一个普通的相机都能够将这个世界所有的物象轮廓非常清晰的记录下来。我注意到，头两天就到达威尼斯的温成，在码头与接待厅来回穿梭进行他的拍摄工作。温成作为威尼斯展览工作队伍中的一员非常偶然，有一天，他电话告诉我："我是温成，吕澎，我听说了你们在威尼斯的展览'给马可波罗的礼物'，这个计划很伟大，我很有兴趣，是否可以让我来为你们做一个纪录片？"我记不清楚谁是温成，可是，我从口音感知到这是一个外国人，但是，突兀的要求让我一时没有判断。我告诉他，你做一个计划吧，我看看具体你能够做什么。很快，他通过 e-mail 将他的想法告诉了我，这个时候，我想起来了，我在展望个人展览的晚餐上见过温成，我的印象中他是一个很勤勉的拍摄者，那种工作的敏捷状态很容易让人产生信任。所以，当我一读到他的 e-mail 中的说明与计划，我就立即给他回复了意见，同意他为"给马可波罗的礼物"展览制作一个专题片。事实上，温成在昨天就开始了他的采访，他抓住 Umberto Vattani 不放，结果导致 Umberto Vattani 为他的采访改变了其他行程的安排。在几天的工作准备与进行中，温成的工作态度和状态给我留下深刻印象，在 San Servolo 的食堂、花园、咖啡厅；在威尼斯的水中、圣马可广场、小巷、餐馆，我们都能够见到他的身影，他按照自己的习惯，顺着自己敏感性，跟踪拍摄、组织采访，他总是以一种跳跃性的姿态在人群里面穿梭，哪怕是

could have captured the outlines of objects around us quite clearly. I noticed Wen Cheng, who had arrived in Venice during the first couple of days, scurrying from dock to exhibition hall as he carried out his photographic work. Wen Cheng became a member of our work team in Venice by chance. One day he called me on the phone: "Lü Peng, I am Wen Cheng. I hear you are in Venice putting on the 'Gift to Marco Polo' exhibit. What an admirable project! I'm happy to hear about it. Can you let me come and make a documentary about it?" I could not remember who Wen Cheng was, but from his accent I could tell he was a foreigner. This request came suddenly, and I could not make a judgment right away. I told him, "Draw up a proposal, and I'll see what I can have you do." Very quickly he sent an e-mail telling me about his concept for a documentary. At that point I recalled that I had seen Wen Cheng at the opening dinner of the "Outlook" exhibition. My impression was that he was an industrious photographer. His nimble way of working gave people confidence in his ability. So when I read his e-mailed proposal, I sent a response back agreeing that he could do a special feature on "A Gift to Marco Polo." In fact, Wen Cheng had begun doing interviews the day before. He had grabbed hold of Umberto Vattani, and as a result Umberto had to re-arrange his schedule for the day. During several days of preparatory work, and then the exhibition itself, Wen Cheng's work attitude and flair made quite an impression on me. In the cafeteria at San Servolo, in the garden, in the café, along the waterways of Venice, on Piazza San Marco, in alleys and restaurants, we would see him flitting in and out of view. According to his own feel for the situation, he trailed behind us shooting footage or arranged interviews. He threaded his way through the crowd in a spontaneous way. Even at the end of a meal he would not pass up a chance to ask an Italian girl what she liked about Chinese art. In this way he turned up much amusing material.

After arranging accommodations, the artists went to the exhibition hall to see the layout. Once they arrived at San Servolo,

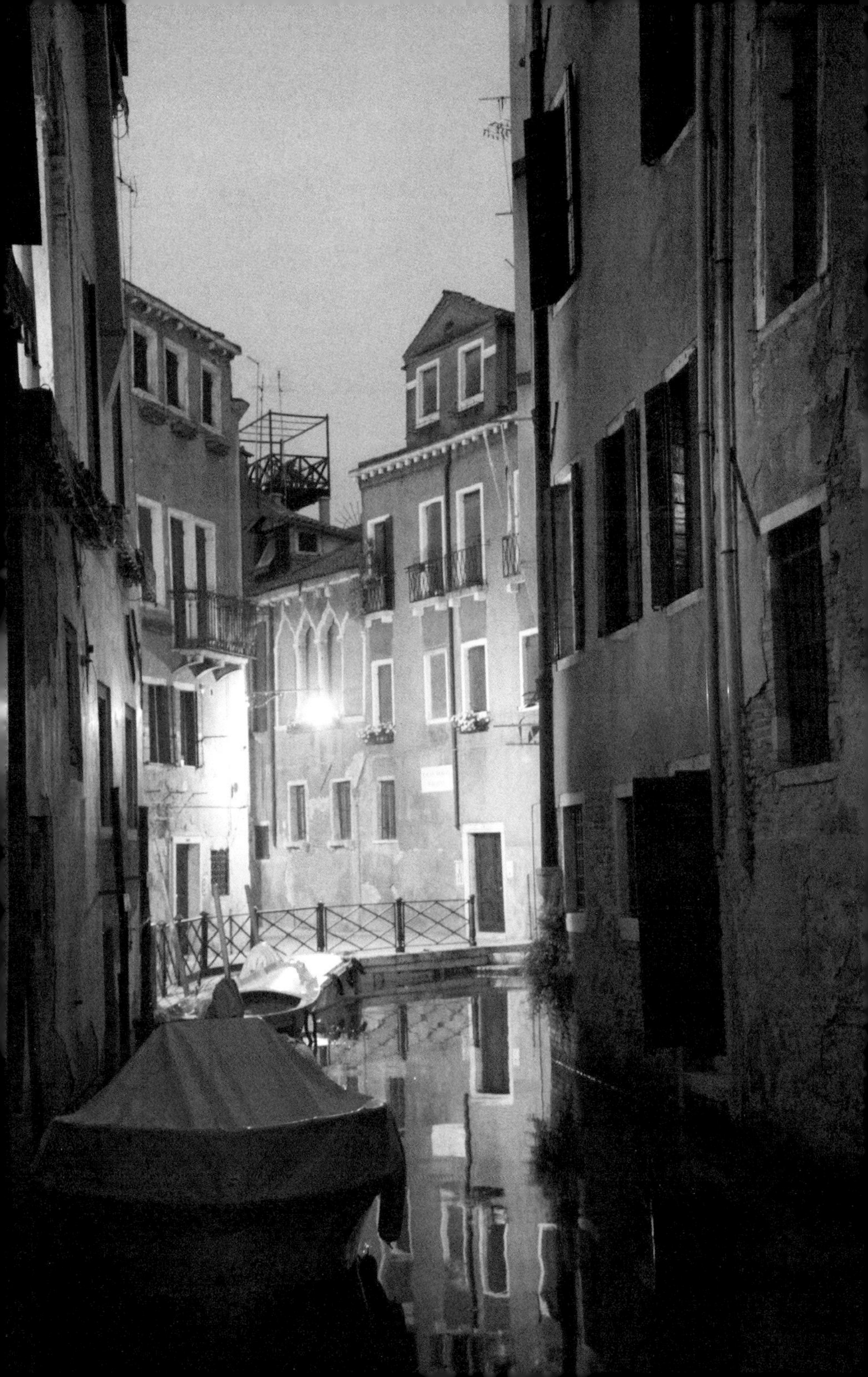

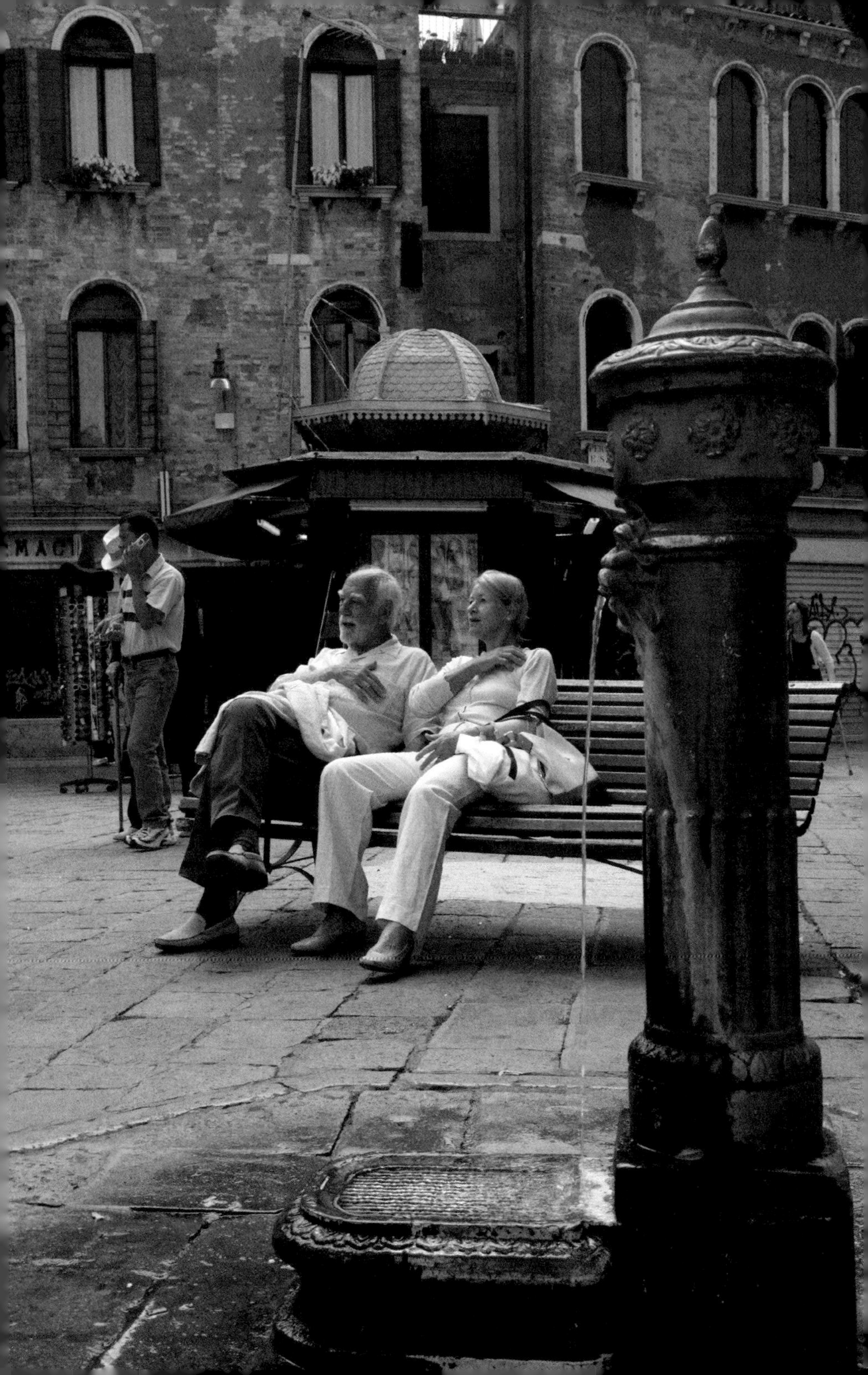

一次晚餐的结束，他也不放弃对一位喜欢中国艺术的意大利女孩的追问，以便收获有趣的素材。

在安排了住宿房间之后，艺术家们到展厅观看作品的布置效果。这天，到达 San Servolo 的人陆续到达本岛，开始了观光。我与朱朱单独在那些小巷里游历。我与朱朱是04年在南京认识的，记得我们在一辆朋友的车里，他似乎很客气地问了我一些艺术圈里的问题。之前，我已经读过朱朱的文字。不过，他与徐累合作的那本可以变成两本的书没有给我很好的印象。在北京丽都广场的咖啡座，洪磊把他们的书《空城记》给我看，我翻了翻，觉得设计很讲究，不过，当时认为内文似乎有些矫饰。洪磊立即拨弄电话给徐累将我的看法转达过去，对方回答似乎有些模棱两可，我要承认，在没有认真阅读的前提下，任何人的意见也只能当作闲暇无聊时的一丝玩笑。后来，我读到了很多朱朱写的艺术家的文字，那些文字非常具有阐释性，分析很丰富，文笔很好，我想，那一定是朱朱诗歌写作的经历所赋予的。通常说，我不太喜欢艺术批评过分的阐释，可是，朱朱的文字倒不属于过分阐释的那一种，而是一种叙事，他在介绍艺术家的经历和分析作品时，总是通过文字引申出更加有内容的联想，这些联想不怎么抽象，倒有些文学性的描述，让人觉得很惬意。这么多年，批评家的批评文章，文字枯燥乏味，装神弄鬼，很难阅读。在我看来，一篇涉及艺术或者艺术家的介绍或者分析文字，需要三个主要的特点：上下文描述、观念阐释以及好的文笔。朱朱的文字给我的深刻印象是他有很好的文笔。当然，没有什么语词是可以自足的，除非她是一种思想的表达，否则这个语词是没有意义的。我承认朱朱的语词是在很美的文笔中组织的，这意味着这些"很美的文笔"包含着观念的阐释以及思想的上下文。朱朱的文字中关于社会与现实的上下文描述很少，这是他的特点，这一定是习惯直指心灵的诗歌文字的诗人长期习惯的结果。何况，过多的社会与现实上下文的描述同样容易导致不着问题的边际。我觉得，朱朱的长处，正好是我的短处，朱朱的文字在感觉中让我联想到波德莱尔 (Charles Pierre Baudelaire)、艾吕雅 (Paul Eluard) 那档档法国人的趣味，尽管他的文字与之并不沾边，无论如何，他的文字给我很好的印象。结果，我们于2008年在湖南美术出版社的圣之空间联合策划了一个联体展览《个案——艺术史中的艺术家》和《个案——艺术批评中的艺术家》，在合作与交往中，渐渐成

the group members began trickling over to the main island to see the sights. Zhu Zhu and I went walking through alleys on the main island, just the two of us. I first met Zhu Zhu in 2004 in Nanjing. I remembered riding with him in a friend's car as he politely asked me questions about the art community. Before that I had already read something by him. However, the book on which he collaborated with Xu Lei, which could be read front-to-back or back-to-front, did not give me a good impression. While having coffee at Lidu Square, Hong Lei showed me a copy of their book—*Empty City Stratagem*. I leafed through it and felt that it was nicely designed, but at the time I felt that the text was somewhat contrived. Right away Hong Lei called Xu Lei on his cell phone to relay my opinion, and Xu Lei's response was somewhat ambiguous. I must admit that without a serious reading, any person's comments on a book should only be taken as amusing banter. Later I read writings on many artists by Zhu Zhu. I found them to contain valuable interpretations; their analyses were multilayered and the style was good. I think that Zhu Zhu's experience with writing poetry must have given him the ability to do these things. Usually I do not like too much interpretation in art criticism, but Zhu Zhu's interpretations do not strike me as overdone. Rather, they present a kind of narrative; in addition to introducing the artist's experience and analyzing the works, his words always invoke substantive associations. These associations are not overly abstract. Instead, they offer a somewhat literary description that is pleasurable to the reader. For quite a few years the writings of Chinese critics have been marred by dry flavorless writing and grandiosity that makes them hard to read. As I see it, a piece of writing that introduces or analyzes art or artists needs to have three features: description of context, conceptual interpretation, and good literary style. I am impressed by the style of Zhu Zhu's writings. Of course, no words can stand on their own, at the risk of being meaningless, unless they succeed as expressions of pure thought. When I avow that Zhu Zhu's words are woven into a beautiful style, this signifies that his style incorporates in-

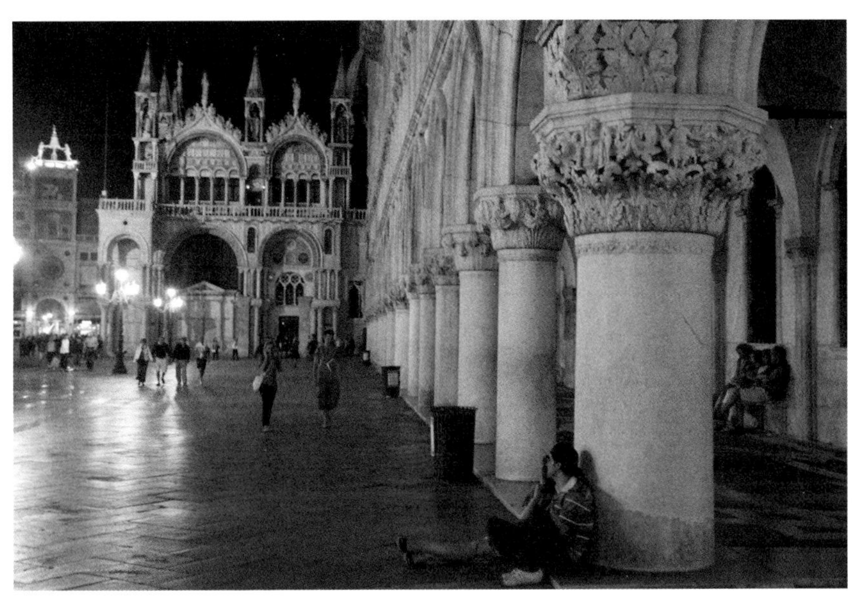

为相互很信任的朋友。

　　下午，我俩在圣马可广场与大队伍碰头小坐之后，就去了 Rialto 桥观看桥下和远处的风景。Rialto 是威尼斯的历史象征，她曾经是连接这个城市的两岸的唯一桥梁，我在这个桥头上已经有了无数次观看，可是我承认，Rialto 具有神秘的力量，让我每一次都有看不够的感觉，我突然联想到了2月里雨水中的 Rialto 周边的景致，那时人们在用扳子搭的路桥上穿梭，没有丝毫觉得别扭。尽管新闻报纸关于威尼斯遭遇严重水灾有充分的报道，但是，在这里游历的人们似乎觉得这是威尼斯天然的风景中的一部分，表现出适应与欣赏，没有觉得什么不妥。

　　黄昏中，我与朱朱在一个安静的小巷边的意大利餐馆晚餐。我们讨论艺术与学术问题；讨论男人与女人；……一包万宝路香烟就在晚餐中结束了。结账时，路灯已经亮了（这个季节的威尼斯要在晚上9点之后才渐渐黑暗），我们回到了圣马可广场，再次选择了一处有音乐的咖啡处坐下来，倾听那些不会让人疲倦的旋律。这个时候，我多少想到在成都茶馆听围鼓的情景，按照描述的习惯，人们爱用"高雅"去描述西方古典音乐，而总是，至少我周边的一些朋友，也总是认为像川剧，尤其是日常茶馆里的围鼓，是俗气的。真的是这样吗？过去我是这么认为的。可是，

terpretation and intellectual context. In Zhu Zhu's writing you will not find much description of social and real-world context. This is something unique about him, and it surely results from a poet's long-cultivated facility at pointing directly to the human heart. What is more, too much description of social and real-world context can cause critics to miss the mark in terms of artistic issues. I feel that Zhu Zhu's strong point is at the same time his weak point. The way Zhu Zhu writes reminds me of expressions of taste by Frenchmen like Baudelaire and Éluard, even though his style does not imitate theirs. At any rate, I was impressed with his writing. As a result, we mounted a joint exhibition through Hunan Fine Arts Press and Shengzhi Art Space. My part was *Case Studies: Artists in Art History*; Zhu Zhu's part was *Case Studies: Artists in the Eyes of a Critic*. In our collaborative exchanges, we gradually came to trust each other as friends.

In the afternoon we two met with the main group at Piazza San Marco and sat for a while, then went to the Rialto to view the scenery under the bridge. The Rialto is a historical symbol of Venice and was once the only bridge linking the two banks of the city. I have surveyed the view from the Rialto numerous times, and I confess that I feel a mysterious power in this bridge and can never get enough of gazing from its side. I was suddenly reminded of the view along the Rialto in the drizzly month of February. Pedestrians were bustling about on plank walkways above the waterline, but they did not show a trace of feeling inconvenienced. Though newspapers had extensive reports of serious flooding in Venice, sojourners here seemed to view this as an innate part of Venice's scenery. They showed adaptability and appreciated the place simply for what it was.

At dusk, Zhu Zhu and I dined at an Italian restaurant beside a quiet alley. We discussed issues of art and scholarship; we also discussed male-female relationships. Between us we finished a pack of Marlboros over dinner. By the time we paid the check, the street lamps were already lit. (During this season Venice does not get dark until after 9:00 p.m.). We went back to Piazza San

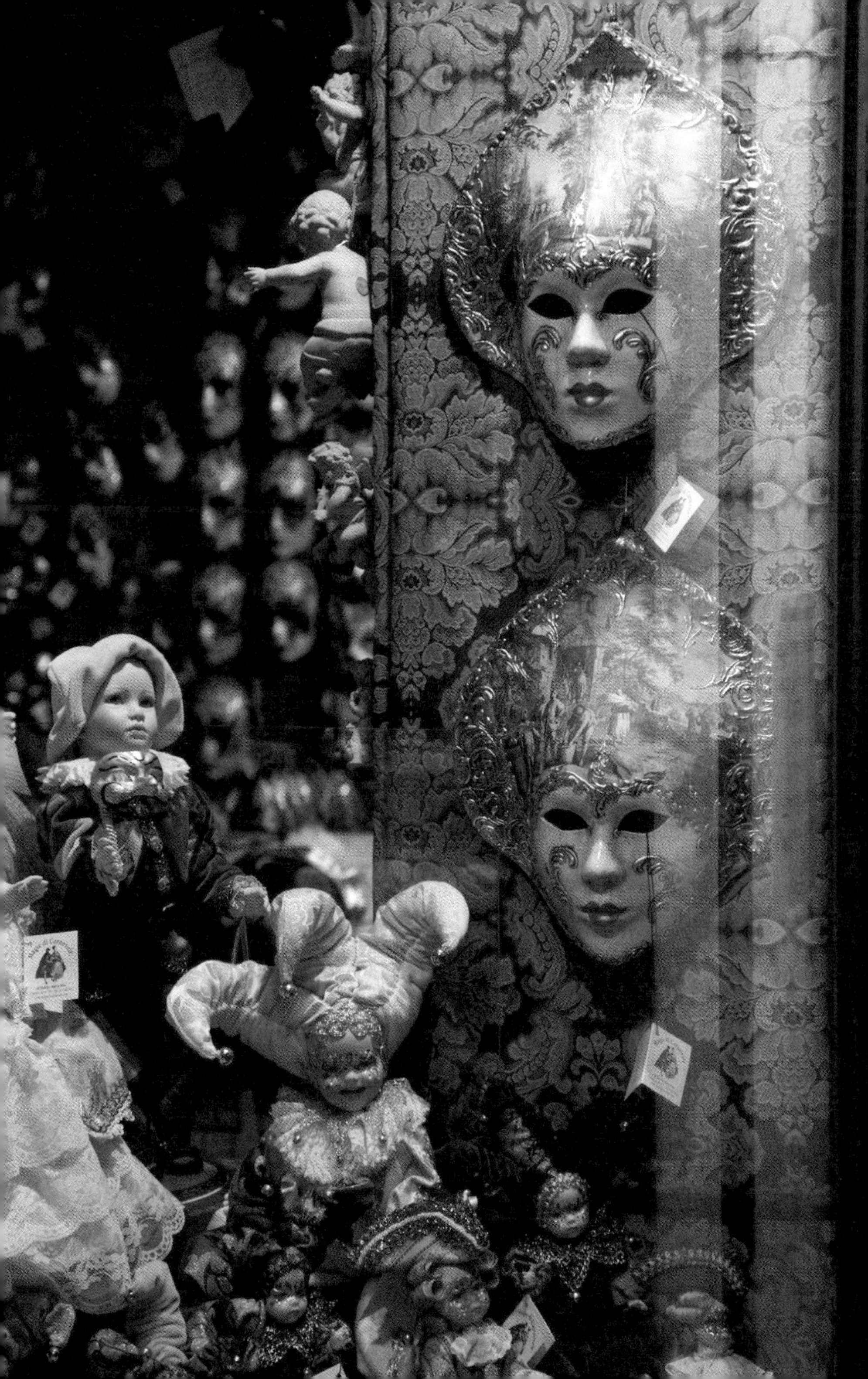

Marco, once again chose a café that had music, and sat listening to those melodies that I never grow tired of. At that point I had memories of sitting in a Chengdu teahouse listening to *weigu* performers. Many people habitually describe Western classical music as "elegant." For the most part, at least in my circle of friends, the vernacular genres of Sichuan opera and the common *weigu* performances in teahouses are considered vulgar. Is it really so? I thought so in the past. But on this particular evening, even while listening to "elegant" Western music, I could easily understand that different contexts lead to different perceptions. If Western performers in formal attire were plunked down to perform in a Suzhou garden or a Chinese teahouse, perhaps we would not feel very comfortable about it. This is true in all manner of things: context is vital. If we pay attention to details, it will be easy to affirm that the system of each civilization has its own importance, and we cannot lightly talk of fusion. We can venture back and forth between the systems of different civilizations, but we should not need to break apart the internal configuration of any one civilization. Apparently postmodernism has not considered such things. It takes truly sensitive, creative people to grasp what truly might be involved in "fusion," despite all the mingling and appropriation that has been popular in recent years.

Leaving the center of the square, we walked along the portico viewing the nighttime Piazza San Marco. At a café near the Piazza exit, everything except the small bandstand was unlit, but a middle-aged couple was dancing to the music. The seating area was almost empty, but that did not affect the dancers' enthusiasm in the slightest. They only needed music, not an audience.

At Dock 20 we waited for a boat back to San Servolo. Wu Shanzhuan sent me a text message: "Heaven's messenger Xiao Quan took wonderful photos." I knew that San Servolo at night with "TOBUY IS TOCREATE" in red neon would make a fine sight. As a member of a Venetian merchant family, Marco Polo would surely be pleased.

今天晚上，即便我正在异国他乡倾听"优美的"西方音乐，也很容易理解：不同的语境总是有不同的感受，如果将那些着装讲究的西方表演者放在苏州园林或者中国茶馆里面演出，也许我们会有不舒服的感觉，任何事情都是这样，语境非常重要。只要我们注意细节，就很容易肯定，文明的系统是如此地重要，不要轻易地去说"融合"，我们可以在不同的文明系统中游历，但是我们没有必要打破她们内部的逻辑关系。后现代似乎没有顾及这些，可是，那些敏感的创造者也许才真正懂得什么是"融合"，尽管"拼凑"、"挪用"是这么多年流行的方法。

离开广场中心，我们沿着回廊观看夜晚的圣马可，广场出口的一个咖啡馆音乐台下已经非常黑暗，有一对中年夫妇在随着音乐跳舞，其实，那些咖啡座位已经几乎没有客人，但这丝毫没有影响这对舞伴的兴致，他们只需要音乐，不需要观众。

在20号码头等待回 San Servolo 的船只时，吴山专发来了一个短信：天媒肖哥，拍摄成功。我知道了，有 TOBUY IS TOCREATE 霓虹灯的 San Servolo 夜景一定好看，作为威尼斯商人家族成员的马可波罗应该非常高兴。

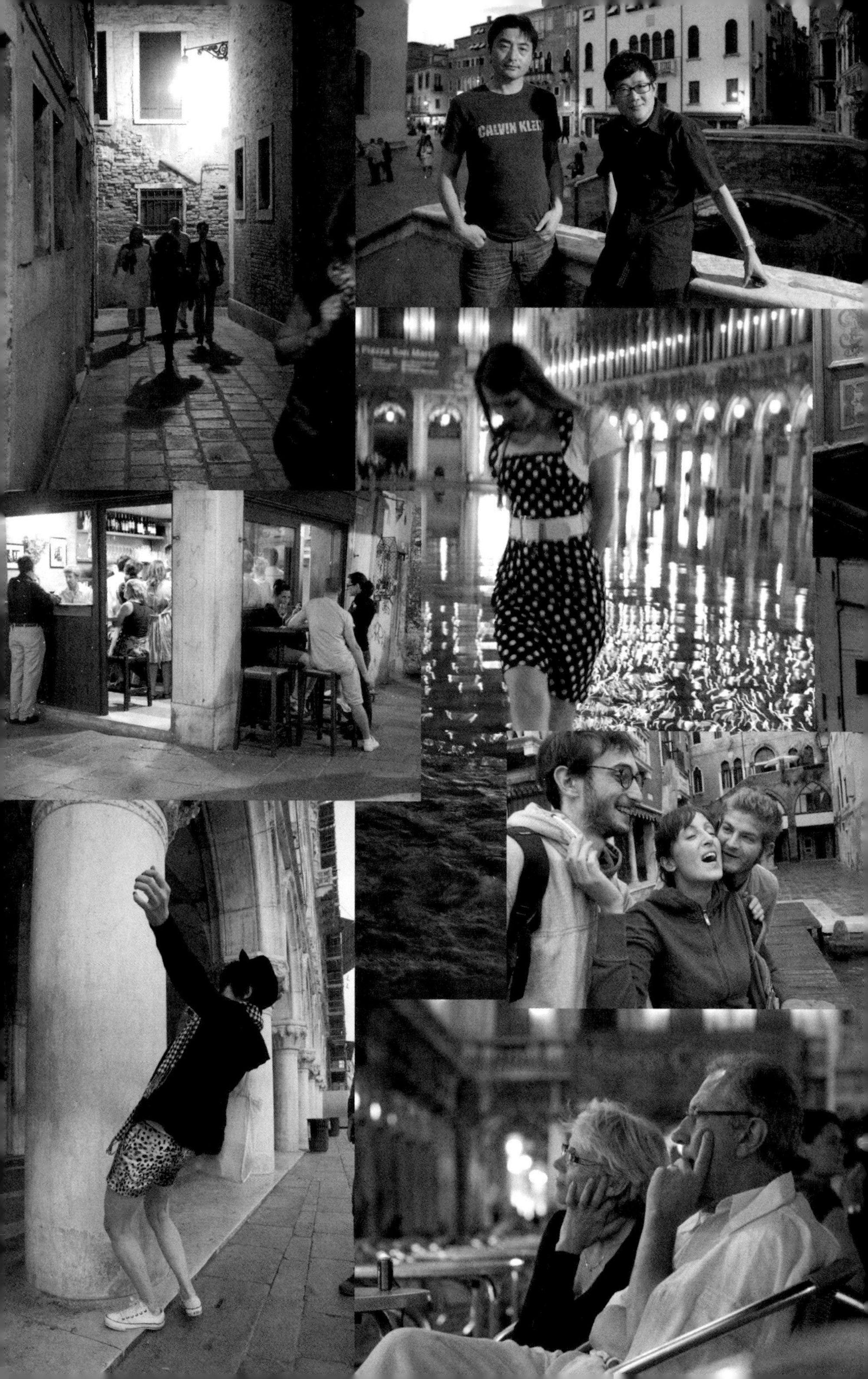

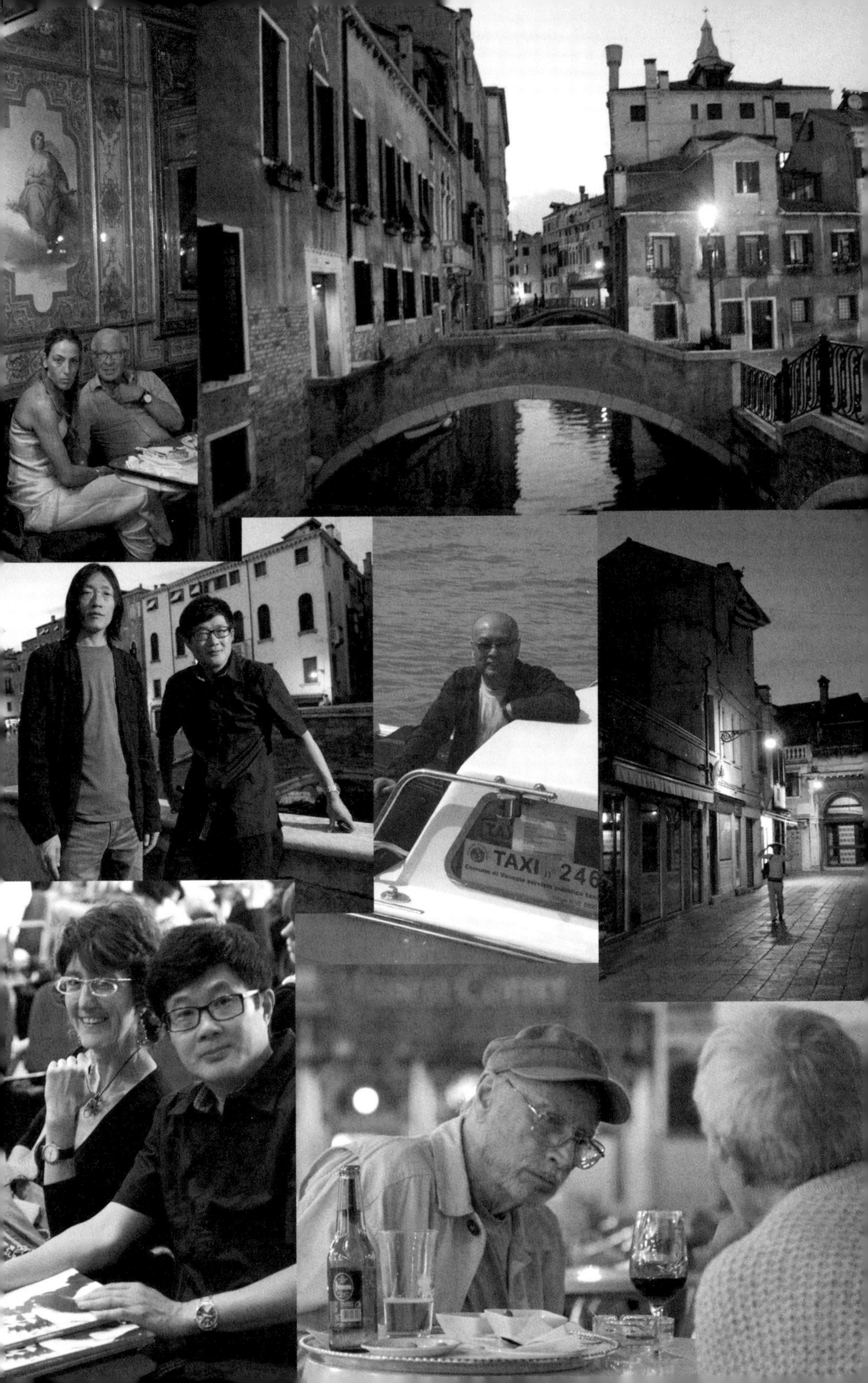

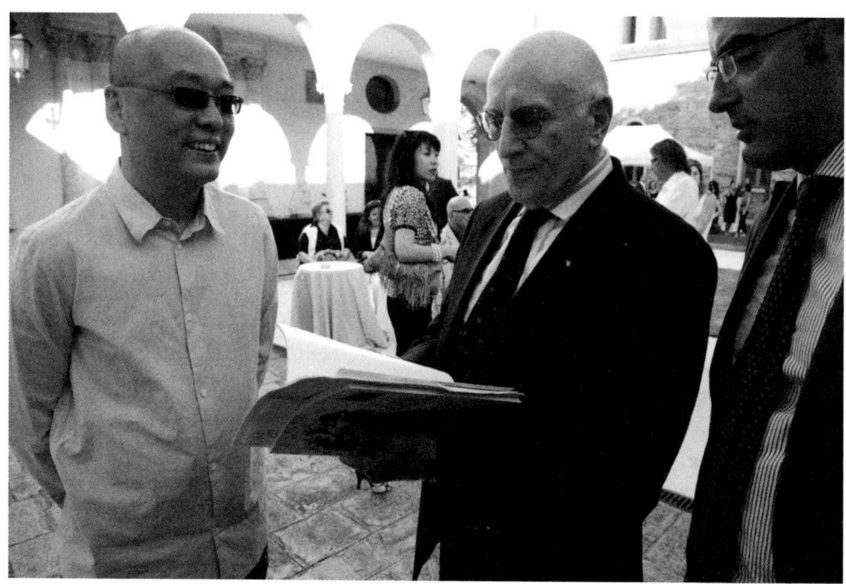# June 2nd

June 2nd was opening day. At around 8:00 that evening Achille Bonito Oliva showed up, accompanied by Umberto Vattani, and greeted the Chinese artists. The Italian critic Oliva was quite familiar with Chinese artists. In 1993 he curated two shows—"Road of the Orient" and "Open-Door Exhibit"—bringing Chinese artists to public notice in Venice for the first time. For Chinese contemporary artists, their first time at the Venice Biennial (the 45th) was quite important. There is no need to tell that story here, for it has become common knowledge in the history of contemporary Chinese art. The critic Li Xianting expressed

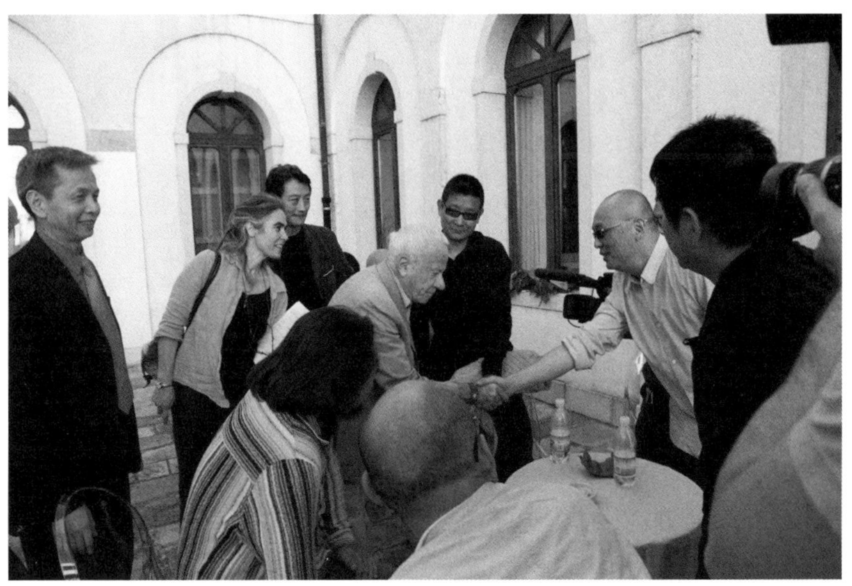

6月2日是开幕式的一天，下午不到8点的样子，奥利瓦 (Achille Bonito Oliva) 来了。他在 Umberto Vattani 的陪同下，来与中国艺术家问好。奥利瓦是中国艺术家非常熟悉的意大利批评家和策展人，他在1993年策划的"东方之路"和"开放展"把中国艺术家第一次带到了威尼斯，带进了国际社会，对于中国当代艺术家来说，这一届（第45届）威尼斯双年展非常重要。这个故事已经不用在这里叙述了，它几乎成为中国当代艺术史的常识。尽管展览之后栗宪庭对奥利瓦的选择仍然不满意，但是，没有这个意大利人，我们的确不知道中国当代艺术会在什么时候出现在国际舞台上，尽管经济的全球化与中国的市场经济终究会把中国当代艺

dissatisfaction in retrospect over Oliva's selections; nevertheless, had it not been for this Italian curator, the appearance of contemporary Chinese art on the global stage would have been delayed for an indefinite period, even though economic globalization and China's market economy would eventually have ushered China's new art onto the world stage. In that same year of 1993, Wang Lin published an article in *Dushu* (issue 10) titled "Oliva Is Not the Savior of Chinese Art," the gist of which was that Chinese contemporary art has its own unique features. A single Italian who is not well versed in Chinese art, no matter who he is, would find it hard to make accurate judgments. The interest in political pop and cynical realism was only a Western perspective or perhaps an ideological strategy. Thus Chinese art's development cannot be entrusted to a Westerner like Oliva. However, he quoted the words of Li Xianting, the shot-caller among Chinese critics, saying, "Even so, we have no choice. We must adapt to their rules, because this is a Western exhibition." Perhaps because of the difficult times people were going through, vigilant types tried to

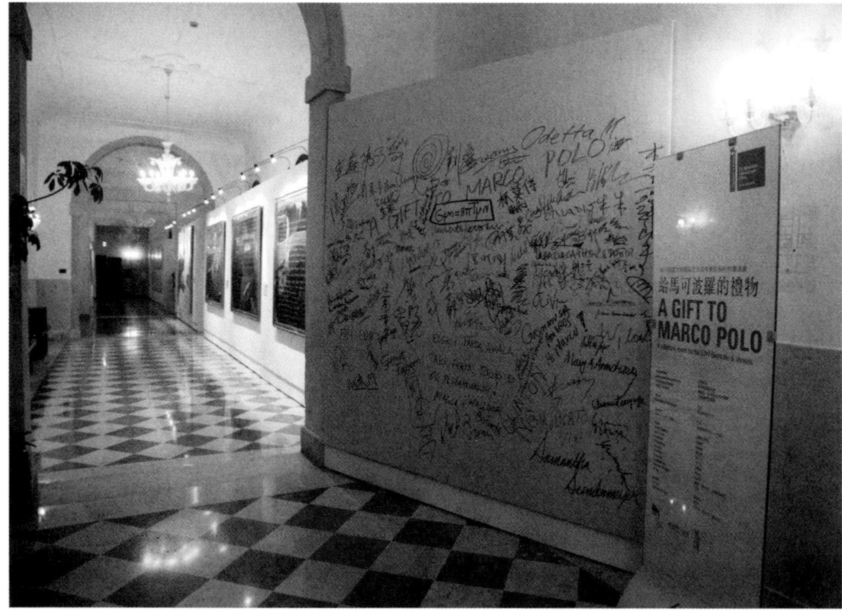

术带到世界中去。就在1993年，王林在《读书》第十期发表了一篇叫做"奥利瓦不是中国艺术的救星"的文章，他的中心意思是说，中国当代艺术有其自身的特殊性，仅仅一个不了解中国的意大利人，无论他是谁，难以有准确的判断，对政治波普和玩世现实主义的兴趣，不过是西方的视角和意识形态策略而已。所以，中国艺术的发展不能寄托在奥利瓦这样的西方人身上。不过，他引用了中方召集人栗宪庭的话："然而我们没有办法，我们必须适应他们的规则，因为这是西方的展览。"也许那是一个艰难岁月，警觉者天生有一个提防的心理，紧张中国的艺术史被西方人乱写，紧张自己丧失了"决策"的权力，在2002年的时候，年龄很大的批评家贾方舟还是这样说，"真正了解中国当代艺术的价值的、并能对它作出深刻阐释的只有中国的批评家。我们不能把中国当代艺术的希望寄托在西方的批评家和策展人身上。我们只有自己救自己。靠中国的批评家来扶持中国的当代艺术。"不过，时间到了2009年的今天，那些唠唠叨叨的批评家还没有认真地说出，除了被西方选中的那些艺术家外，哪些中国艺术家的艺术可以体现出中国当代艺术的价值？这时间可是已经过了十五、六年了，警惕被西方颠覆的心理状态直到今天也没有消失，很多批评家至今也是这样看待中国当代艺术的状况的。"西方阴谋论"成为时尚术语，让那些如此判断者高兴得不行。

我一直不是很在意这样的问题，作为有独立人格的人，我们有什么样的艺术判断就拿出来，不必有太多的顾虑与警惕。所以，当 Umberto Vattani 推荐奥利瓦来做意方策展人时，我很高兴，能够与这个老头合作一下，不是很好吗？他也是人啊！一个意大利人，一个对诗歌和艺术具有洞察力的人，一个对中国当代艺术有所作为的人。他的英语讲得不是很好，所以只能简单地与大家聊天，Umberto Vattani 很快就开始组织奥利瓦与艺术家们合影，在合影的过程中，奥利瓦把易英翻译的他写的两本书《叛逆的思想》和《马塞尔杜尚的一生》送给了我。我觉得他很友好，挺有趣的。

开幕式是在8点过十分开始的。首先是 Umberto Vattani 发表了热情洋溢的讲话，我知道，Umberto Vattani 是真的喜欢中国和中国文化的，尽管他年纪很大了，但是，他精力充沛，思维十分敏捷，最让我吃惊的是，在我们2月访问期间晚上听音乐会的时候，他居然在等待开幕的前十几分钟里，在纸上已经将整

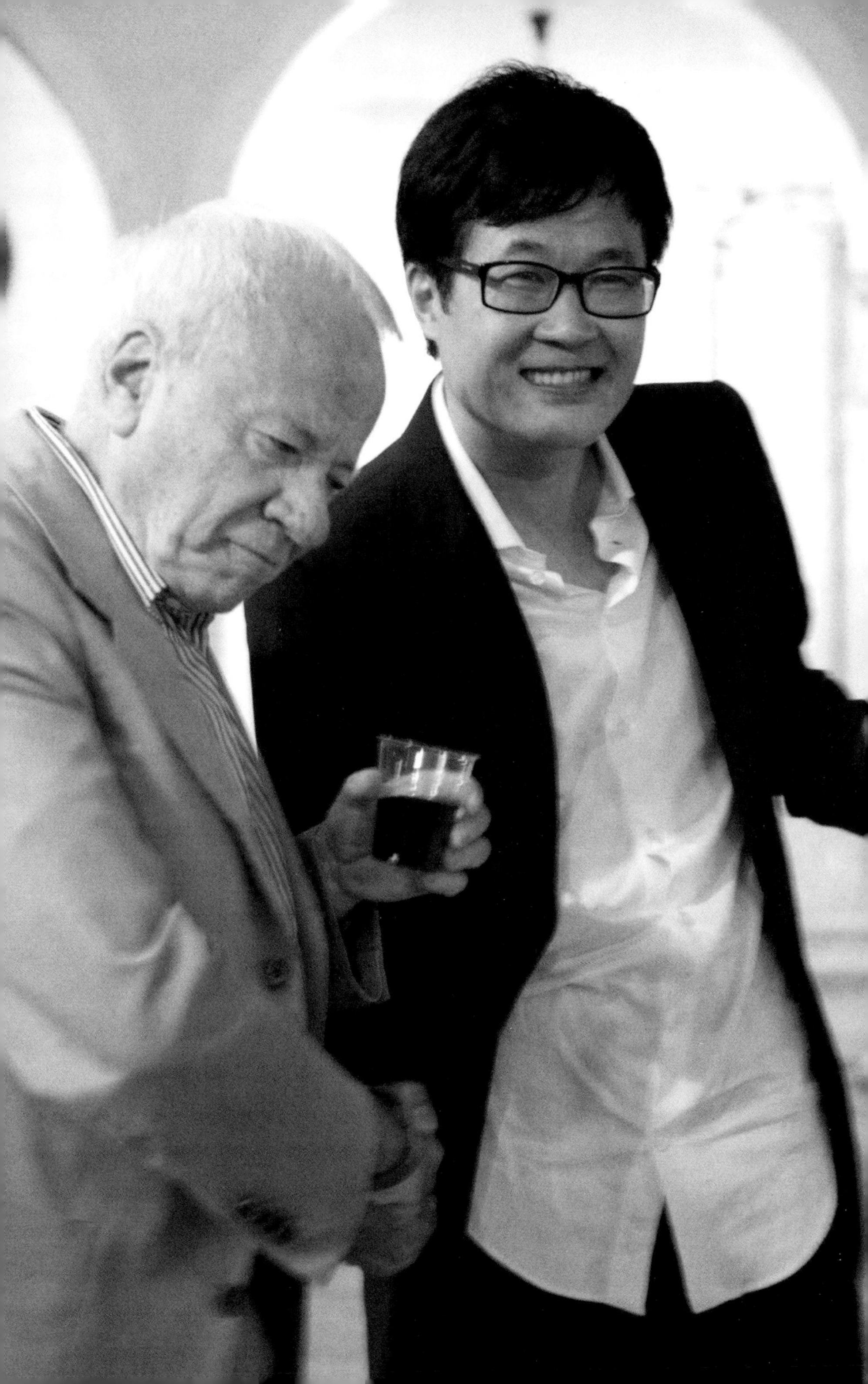

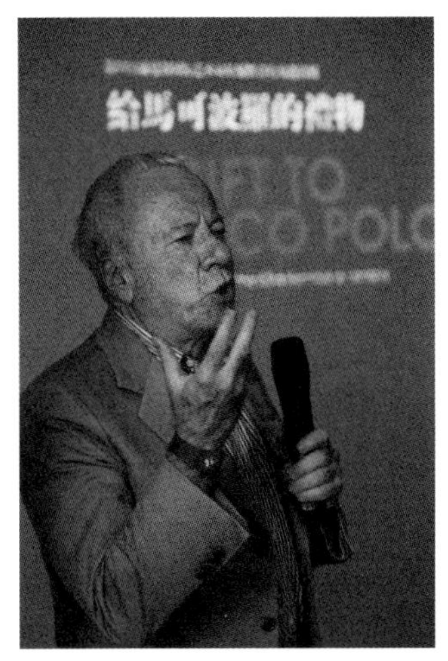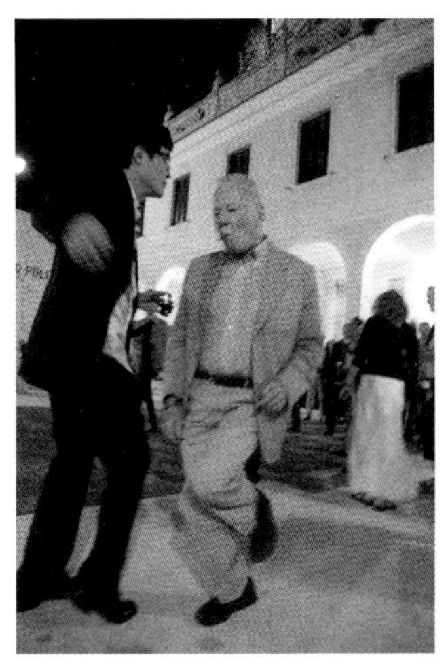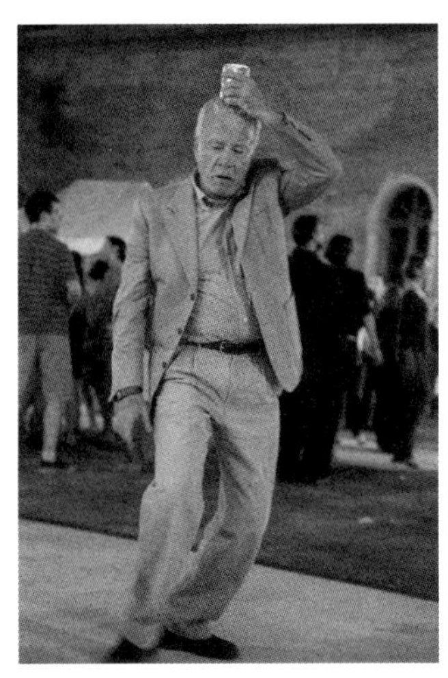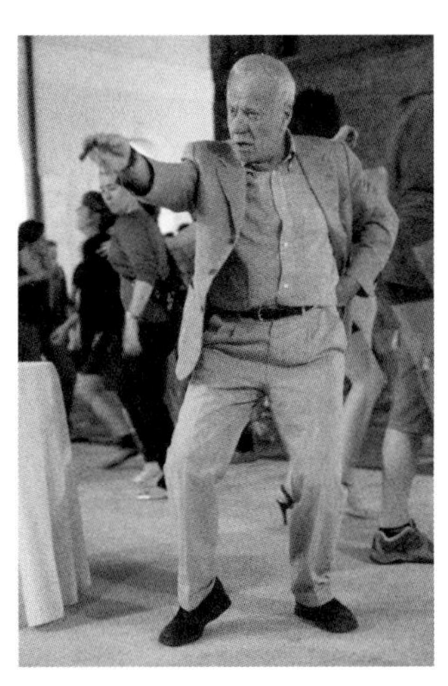

个展览的安排与策划勾勒清楚，他还将开幕式的程序作了考虑，他在整整一张纸上密密麻麻地写下那些层次清楚的文字，让我非常感动。尽管12月26日接受参加展览的申请时间早就过去，也正是 Umberto Vattani 的努力，使得本次展览作为双年展的一部分成为可能。我用吃力的英文向在场的嘉宾说明了展览的策划思想，并一一介绍了艺术家和他们的作品。接着就是奥利瓦即兴发言，他一会是意大利语，一会又用英文，我没有太听得懂他的意思，不过，他开玩笑地说，今天，我与他重新构成了忽必烈和马

arm themselves psychologically, being apprehensive that Chinese art history would be miswritten by Westerners. They were wary lest they lose their own decision-making authority. In 2002 the graybeard critic Jia Fangzhou was still saying, "Only a Chinese critic can truly understand the value of contemporary Chinese art and elucidate it in depth. We cannot entrust our hopes for contemporary Chinese art to Western critics and curators. We can only save ourselves; we can only rely on Chinese critics to foster contemporary Chinese art." Yet as of 2009 those pedantic critics have still not seriously stated which artists, excluding those chosen by the West, have created works which reflect the true value of contemporary Chinese art. At least five or six years have gone by, and apprehensiveness over Western subversion has still not faded away. Many critics today still take this view of our contemporary art. The "doctrine of Western conspiracy" has become a fashionable phrase, and it has been gladly adopted by those who make judgments like the above.

I have not paid a great deal of mind to such issues. As people of independent character, let us present our judgments about art whatever they may be. So when Umberto Vattani recommended Oliva as curator on the Italian side, I was happy to hear it. Would it not be a good thing to collaborate with that old gent? He is a human being too! An Italian, a man with insight into poetry and art, a man who has done something for contemporary Chinese art. His spoken English was slow, so he could only make simple conversation with our group. Umberto promptly had him pose for joint photos with our artists. During the photo session, Oliva gave me Italian-English bilingual versions of two books he had written: *Rebellious Thinking* and *Marcel Duchamp: A Life*. I found him to be friendly and amusing.

The opening began at ten minutes past 8:00. Umberto Vattani started things off with an enthusiastic speech. I knew that Vattani was truly fond of China and Chinese culture. Although much older than myself, his energy was abundant and his wit was nimble. Most amazing to me was the time we had gone to a con-

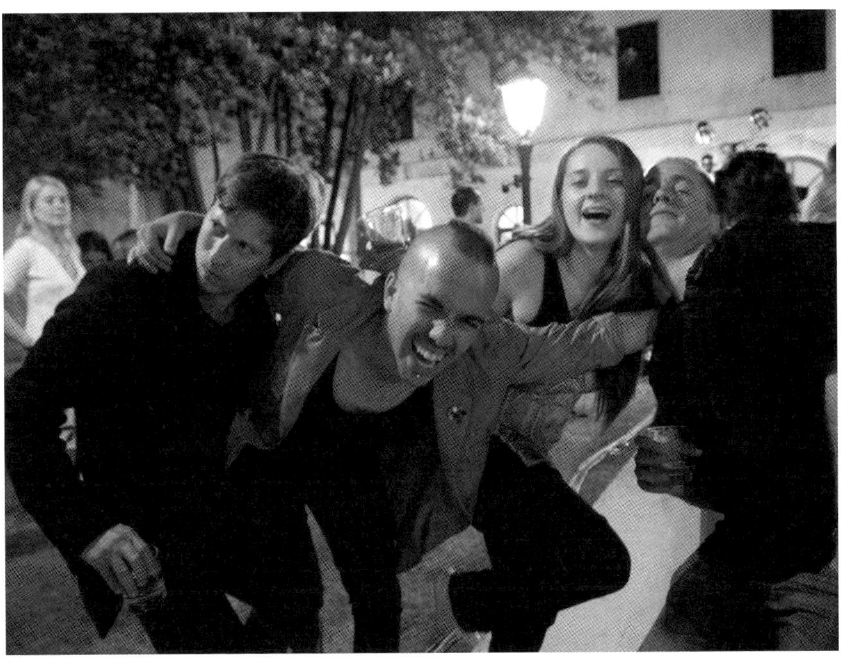

cert together during my survey trip in February. While waiting for the curtain to rise, over the course of a little over ten minutes, he had outlined arrangements for our exhibition. He had even devised a timetable for opening night and filled a sheet of paper densely with his orderly writing. I was quite moved. Although the December 26th deadline to apply for exhibitions had passed, due to Vattani's efforts it became possible for our show to be a part of the Biennial. In careful English he explained our show's curatorial concept to our opening guests. Then one by one he introduced the artists and their works. After that Oliva gave a spontaneous talk, switching back and forth between Italian and English. I did not understand all he said, but I caught a joke—that our meeting today was a re-enactment of the encounter between Kublai Khan and Marco Polo, and that as such it marked a continuing chapter of East-West communication. I did not see his metaphor as an exaggeration, but simply took it as an amusing bit of repartee. Wang Guangyi took the floor next and said he regretted Marco Polo had no chance to see the gift being presented to him, but he trusted that Old Marco's dependents would accept it in his stead and relay the news to their ancestor. After Wang Guangyi spoke we had a bit of ceremony: on behalf of all the artists, Zhang Xiaogang and Ye Fang presented to Umberto Vattani the album leaf they had done jointly on April 9th in Suzhou, featuring ink-brush depictions of rocks, vases, plum blossoms, flowing water, and other very Chinese motifs. That night everyone had drinks, then listened to *pipa* music and *kunqu* opera. The artists also daubed images and characters on three new album leaves. On one of them, each artist calligraphed the words *jingshen* ("spirit"). Each artist scrawled these words casually, imbuing them with his or her own temperament. It was my idea to give the album leaves to Umberto Vattani. I felt that this approach related to our theme: after all this was a gift to Westerners by a group of Asian people. Such an object, which can only find a context in traditional Chinese culture, evinces a unique form of personal cultivation and is thus suited to our message.

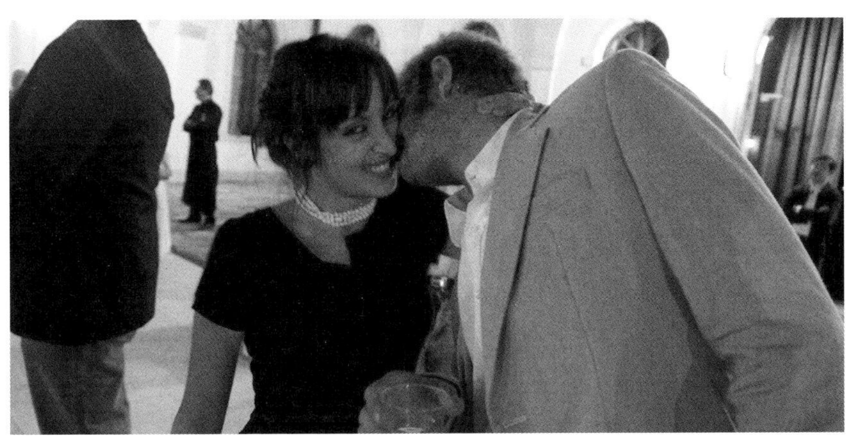

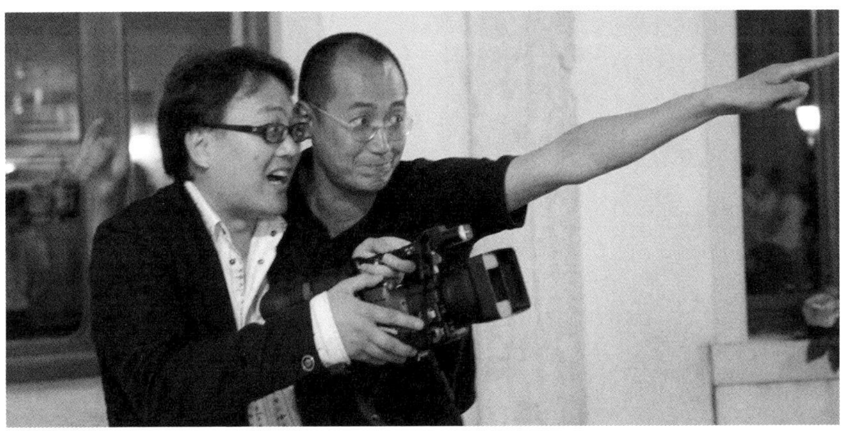

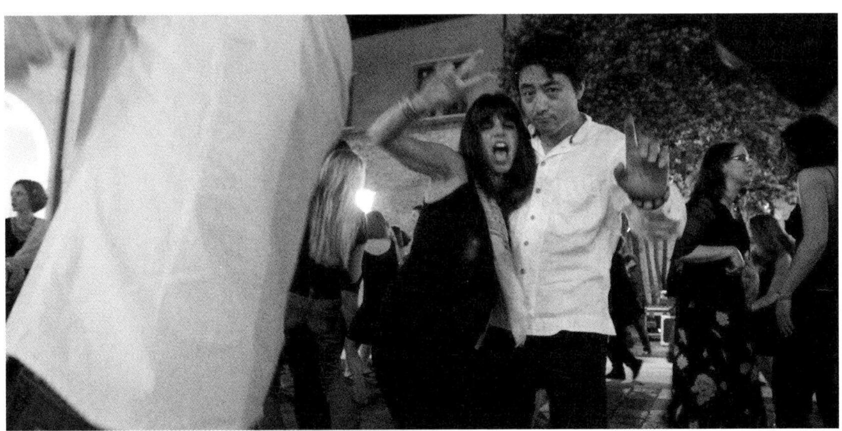

The last speaker was Gong Mingguang [Samuel Kung], director of Shanghai Contemporary Art Museum. He spoke of his plan to hold a joint exhibition for the nine male artists and one female artist here today, to be presented as a metaphor of yin and yang. The next day, at a banquet held for the artists on the main island, Umberto Vattani repeated this metaphor.

The opening ceremony with its speeches was over, and the party got underway. There was much mingling and cocktail chatter among friends and guests. Many of us were amazed by Oliva, who had his own personal style of dancing. We had all had a few drinks. He held a cigar in one hand, and with the other he steadied a cocktail glass atop his head, making a droll spectacle of himself. Xiao Quan was able to catch his memorable dance moves on camera. With glass in hand I danced face to face with him for quite some time. I cannot dance, and I rarely join in on the dance floor, but on this occasion where Italians and other Europeans were in the majority, I felt very casual about dancing—there was no embarrassment or awkwardness. Actually I would not venture to say I was all that happy: I was merely drawing on the intoxicating power of wine and the relaxed setting. There is no way to explain it rationally, except to say that work was finished and I could let myself go.

After the party got underway, Zhang Peili, Huang Zhuan, and Wang Guangyi went back to Building 14. At the party, only Zhang Xiaogang and He Duoling remained, looking on with avid interest. I asked Xiaogang how he felt. He said that although he was not dancing himself, he could feel the vitality and enthusiasm of the occasion. He found the atmosphere enlivening. For many years now Xiaogang has gotten out of the habit of turning in early; he has even become somewhat afraid of solitude and darkness. Of course this is my own individual perception. He did not go back to his own room until quite a late hour.

可波罗的关系，继续着东西方之间的沟通与交流。我没有把他的
这个比喻看成是夸张，而仅仅是理解为和谐气氛的风趣。王广义
接着奥利瓦后面发言，他说，很遗憾，马可波罗没有机会看到今
天中国艺术家送给他的礼物，不过，他相信，老马的后裔会接受
这些礼物，并转告他们的先人。在王广义发言后，有一个小小的
仪式：张晓刚和叶放代表参展艺术家将大家于4月9日在苏州完成
的册页赠送给 Umberto Vattani，那册页上面有十位艺术家用毛
笔画的石头、花瓶、梅枝、流水以及其他非常中国的东西。那天
晚上，大家在酒后倾听琵琶和昆曲，并在三个册页上涂涂画画，
在其中一个册页上，每个艺术家写了"精神"二字，可是，从那
些乱涂的笔迹上，还是可以透露出每个人的气质。将册页送给
Umberto Vattani 是我的主意，我觉得这样的形式与我们的主题
有些联系，毕竟是东方人要送给西方人的礼物，那些只有在中国
传统文化中才能找到上下文的物品，具有特殊的教养与贴切。最
后发言的是上海当代艺术馆馆长龚明光，他将九位男艺术家与一
位女艺术家共同举办展览，比喻为中国的阴阳，次日在本岛宴请
艺术家的午餐上， Umberto Vattani 还重复了这个比喻。

　　开幕式讲话结束了，晚餐 party 开始，来宾与朋友们喝酒聊
天不在话下。让大家吃惊的是，奥利瓦的舞姿很有风格。那是酒
过三旬的时刻，他一只手夹着雪茄，另一只手居然将酒杯顶在头
上，表情颇为诙谐，给大家留下深刻印象，肖全很及时地记下了
这个瞬间。我端着酒杯与他有好一段时间的共舞。我不会跳舞，
凑热闹的情况也很少，可是，在意大利人和欧洲人占多数的场
合，我觉得跳舞变得非常随便，完全没有尴尬与不适。其实，也
谈不上非常高兴，只是借着酒性，借着放松的环境。唯一可以理
性地分析的是，工作已经结束，可以放松自己了。

　　在舞会开始一段时间后，张培力、黄专和王广义回到了14号
楼。现场，只有张晓刚和何多苓很有兴致地观看着。我问刚儿感
受如何？他说，虽然自己不去跳舞，但是，这个场面能够让人感
受到活力与热情，这样的气氛很养人。刚儿已经很多年不习惯早
早睡觉，他甚至害怕单独与黑暗，这当然是我个人的感觉。他直
到很晚才回到自己的房间。

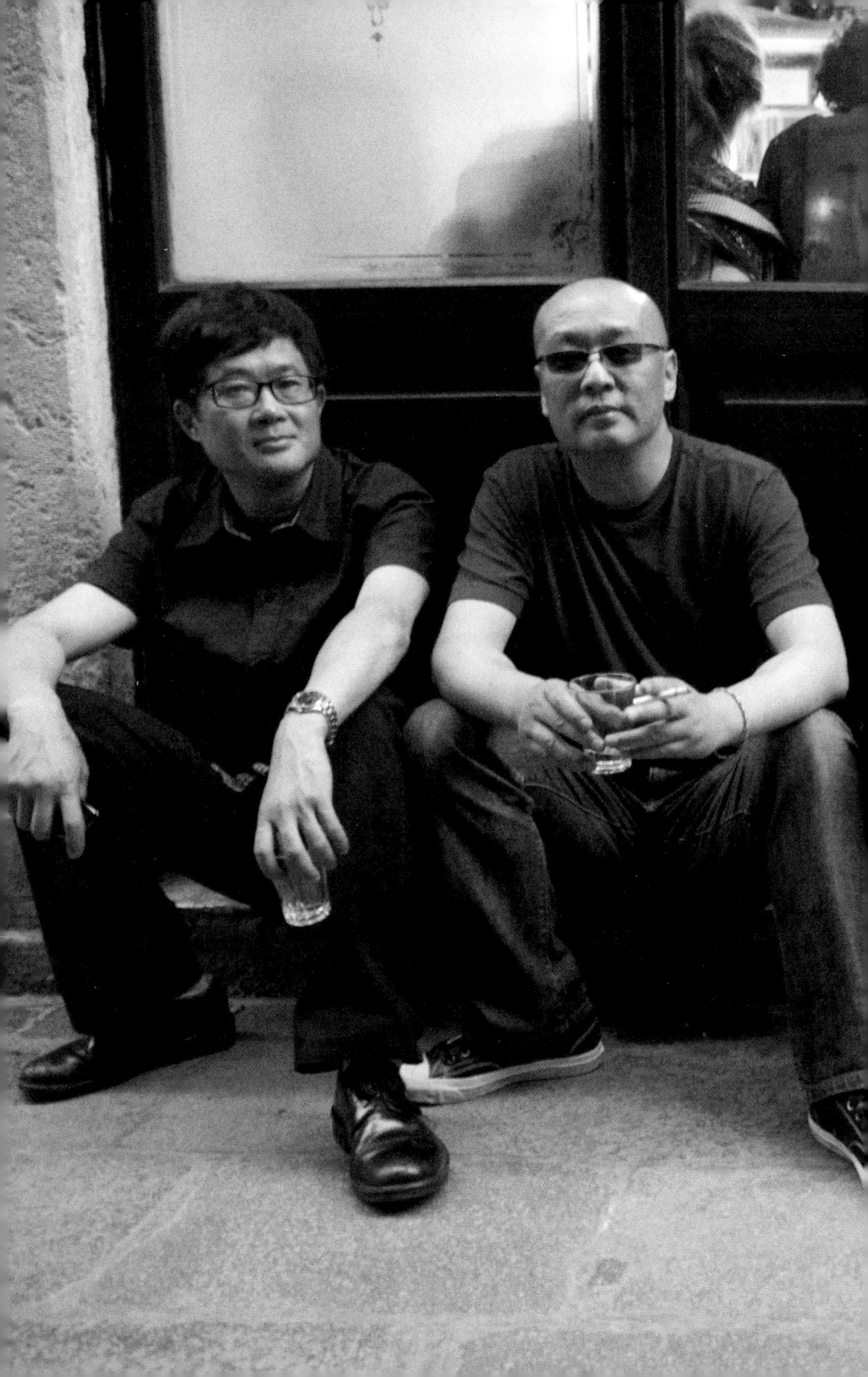

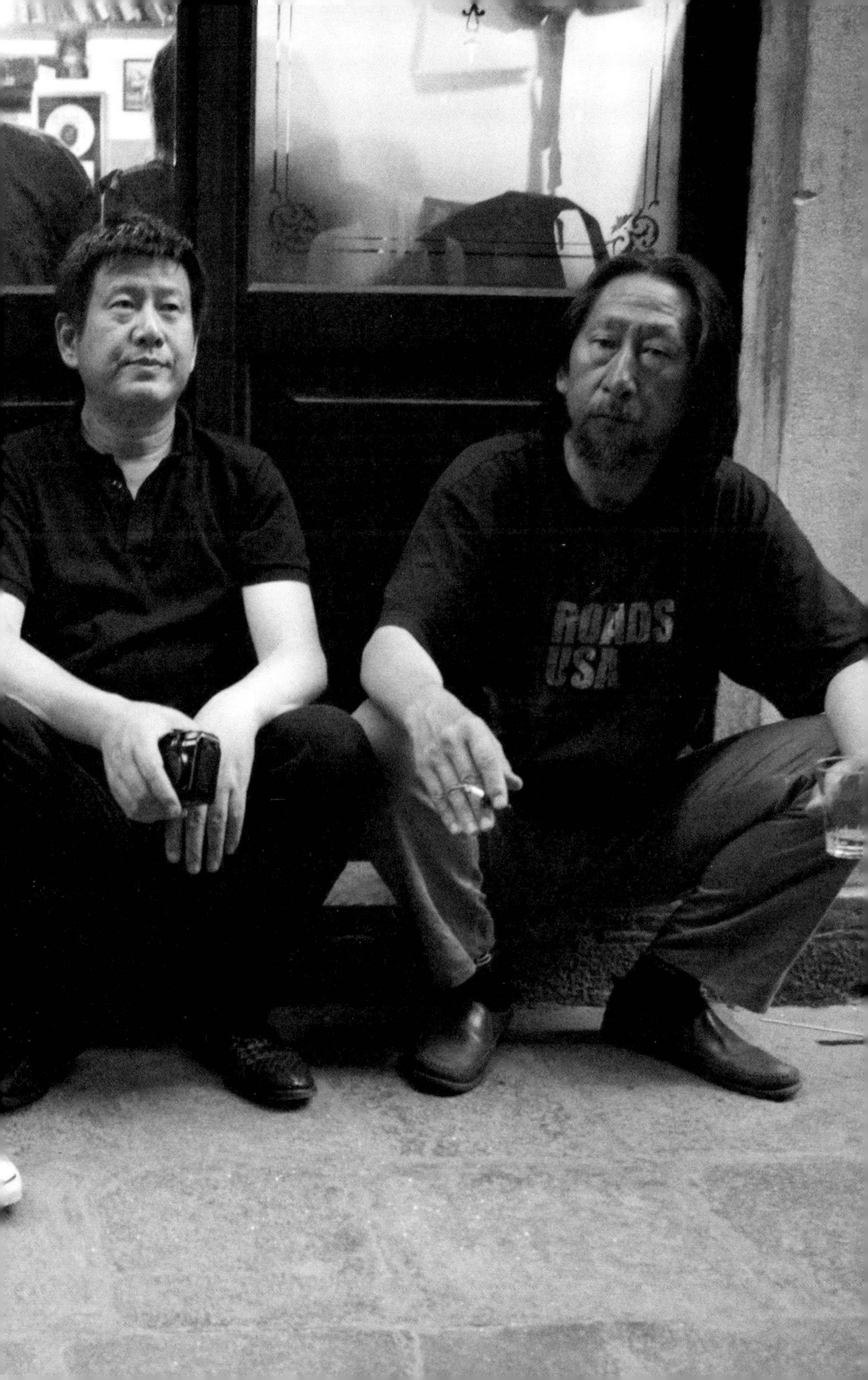
ROADS
USA

June 3rd

Regarding the conference of June 3rd I have few impressions worth noting. But Zhou Chunya's answers to questions from the audience were amusing. One questioner seemed to imply that there was something dubious about this artist's use of dogs as subject matter for so many years. After all this time, once again he was showing dog images in this exhibition. What was one to make of this? Zhou Chunya said, "I feel that Marco Polo would not reject this as a gift." This answer, which I consider witty, drew a laugh from the audience. Even before the exhibition formally started, sightseers were already posing for pictures beside Zhou's dog statue, and children squealed with laughter as they straddled the green dog as if it were a horse. Just before we closed the exhibition, I heard that Zhou's dog was a favorite with many viewers, which gives an idea of its actual value.

Seeing Monica Dematté at the conference was also an event worth recording. I first met the youthful Monica in 1992 in Guangzhou. At that time I only knew that she was Italian and that she liked Chinese art. This was my only notion of her, and I could not fill it in with anything substantive. In ensuing years I saw her a few times and noticed her articles about Chinese art and artists. One day I came upon a book of her collected essays at 798 Modern Bookshop titled *Art, an individual research – my experience of the last twenty years of Chinese art*. Only then did I form an opinion: for all these years Monica has been an inseparable participant in the Chinese art world. I have not read a lot of her articles, but on the strength of what I have seen and heard and

<h1 style="text-align:center">6月3日</h1>

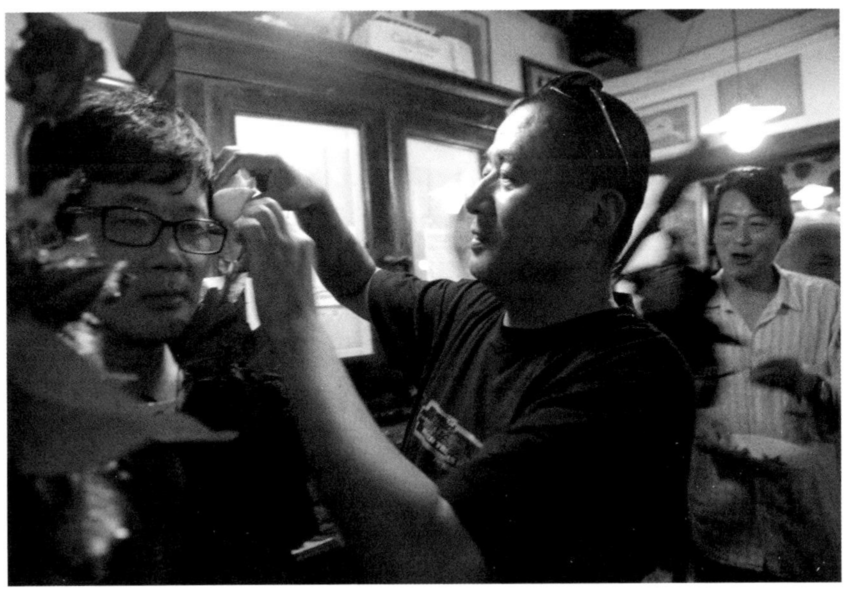

　　我对6月3日的研讨会没有太多值得记录的印象。只是在研讨会上春芽回答台下的提问很好玩，提问者多少有些质疑的暗示，这位中国艺术家用狗做题材的时间已经有很多年了，今天，再次用狗来参加展览意味着什么呢？周春芽回答说："我觉得马可波罗不会反对我送给他的礼物。"台下一片笑声，这个回答的确很智慧的，我觉得。还没有正式展出的时候，就有游客在雕塑边照相，小孩骑在像马一样大的绿狗上开心死了。快撤展的时候，我听说，很多观众对周的狗特别喜欢，其实，这已经很说明问题了。

　　在研讨会上见到了莫尼卡（Monica Dematté）算是一件事情。在1992年的时候，我在广州第一次见到了年轻的莫尼卡，那

read, this is the impression I formed. Time is definitely an unopposable force. Monica is obviously older in appearance, just like the artists that she is familiar with. While the artists were answering questions up on stage, she and I had a short conversation. The exchanges between audience and artists, plus the less-than-fluid renderings of the interpreter, prompted her to chime in with several understated remarks. The most interesting thing she said was that in view of all the Chinese people present, and all of the Chinese works on exhibit, one could say that San Servolo is becoming a Chinese colony. My answer: "Apparently so."

That evening Cheng Xindong hosted a great number of us at a unique restaurant on the main island. An Italian girl who raised two questions during the afternoon conference went along with us. The conference ended, but she looked as if she did not want to leave. She said she was fond of Chinese art, and that she was writing a paper about Wang Guangyi. She said that she was quite happy to see the artist right in front of her eyes. She seemed to have an inexhaustible fund of questions. Under the canopy of a table at the campus café, she asked how a young artist could hope to achieve success. I felt it was a drain of energy to answer such a question, but I told her my opinion. She shot pictures of Chinese artists with her camera in a state of barely suppressed excitement. Before we set out from the San Servolo dock, she seemed reluctant to split up with us. I told her that if she was willing, she could come along with us. And so she became a member of our dinner party. At Piazza San Marco everyone had their picture taken with her. She was definitely an attractive girl, with a breezy manner and plenty of personality. At the table she sat between Guangyi and Xiaogang, which to her was the height of enjoyment. She pulled out her notebook and asked the two artists to draw and write in it. They wrote subtle one-liners and humorous sentences; the images they drew seemed half-alive. Zhang Xiaogang drew a puppy. All this definitely gave her lots of food for thought. That evening Xiaogang made many amusing, deeply insightful remarks, which I attributed to wine and the proximity of a charming woman.

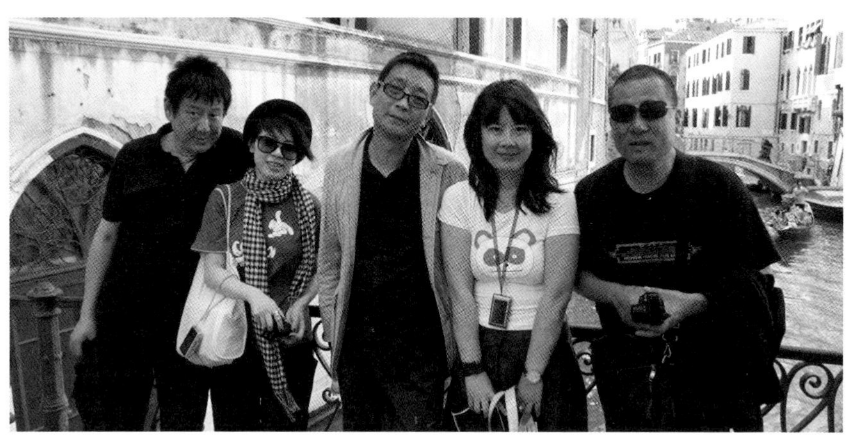

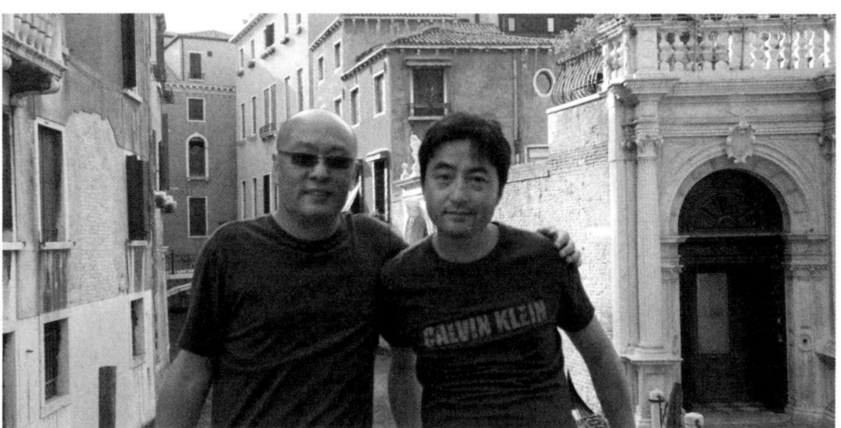

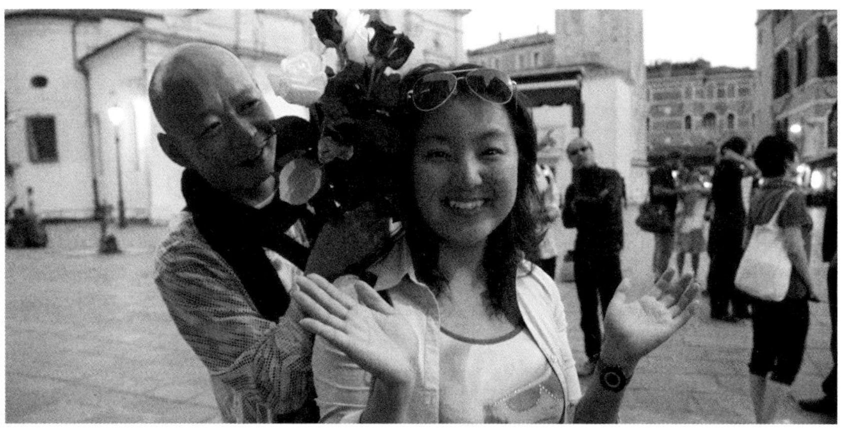

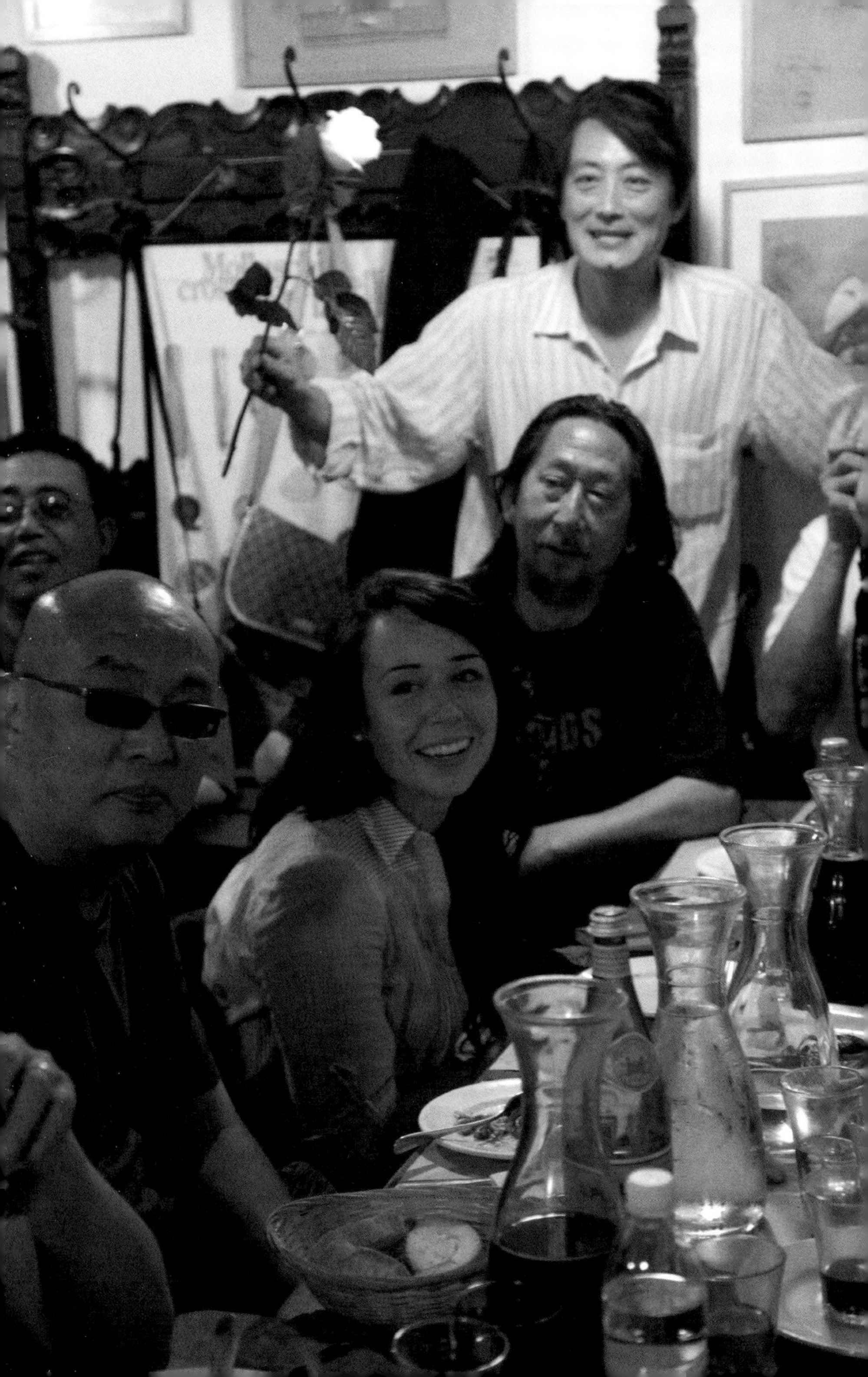

时，我仅仅知道她是意大利人，喜欢中国的艺术。这个印象没有任何价值，不过是一个概念。以后很多年，我也是不多地见到过她，并在杂志上读到了她写的关于中国艺术和艺术家的文章。直至有一天，我在798现代书店里看到了她的文集《艺术：各自为战的运动——亲历中国当代艺术20年》（2008年）的出版，才有了一个看法：莫尼卡是这么多年来的中国艺术难以简单分割的参与者。我没有读过她的多少文章，我仅仅是凭借着不断看到、听到、读到的印象，构成了这样的看法。时间的确具有势不可挡的力量，莫尼卡看上去明显老了，就跟她非常熟悉的那些艺术家一样。当艺术家在台上回答问题期间，我们在下面有一小段时间的交流，台下的提问和台上的回答，以及不是很流畅的翻译，刺激了她不少含蓄的言论，她的最有趣的说法是：这里这么多中国人，又是中国艺术家的展览，所以可以说 San Servolo 已经成为中国的殖民地了。我回答说：看来是。

晚上是程昕东在本岛的一个非常有特点的小店请客。有很多人参加。在下午会议上提出过两个问题的意大利女孩也跟我们一块。会议结束了，可是，我见她没有离开的意思。她说她非常喜欢中国的艺术，她正在写作关于王广义的研究文章，她说她今天居然能够见到艺术家本人，实在是太高兴了。她看上去有很多问题要问，在学校咖啡厅露天的遮阳伞下，她问一个年轻的艺术家如何能够获得成功。我当然觉得回答这样的问题太累，但是也给她说了我的看法。她用自己的相机拍摄中国艺术家，状态有一种抑制不住的兴奋。我们在 San Servolo 码头出发之前，她犹豫着是否跟着我们，我告诉她说，如果你愿意，当然可以。这样，她成为这帮吃饭队伍中的一员。在圣马可广场，大家都跟她一块照相，的确，她漂亮，并且是轻松活泼充满个性的那种。在饭桌上，她坐在广义与刚儿之间，她觉得她实在是享受之至，她拿出自己的笔记本，让这两位中国艺术家在上面写写画画，那其中微妙的语词、幽默的调子以及生动的形象——张晓刚画了一只小狗——一定成为她今后生活与学习的作料。在这个晚上，广义又一次地说出了很多生动有趣、充满智慧的话，我想，那总是酒与女人的结果。

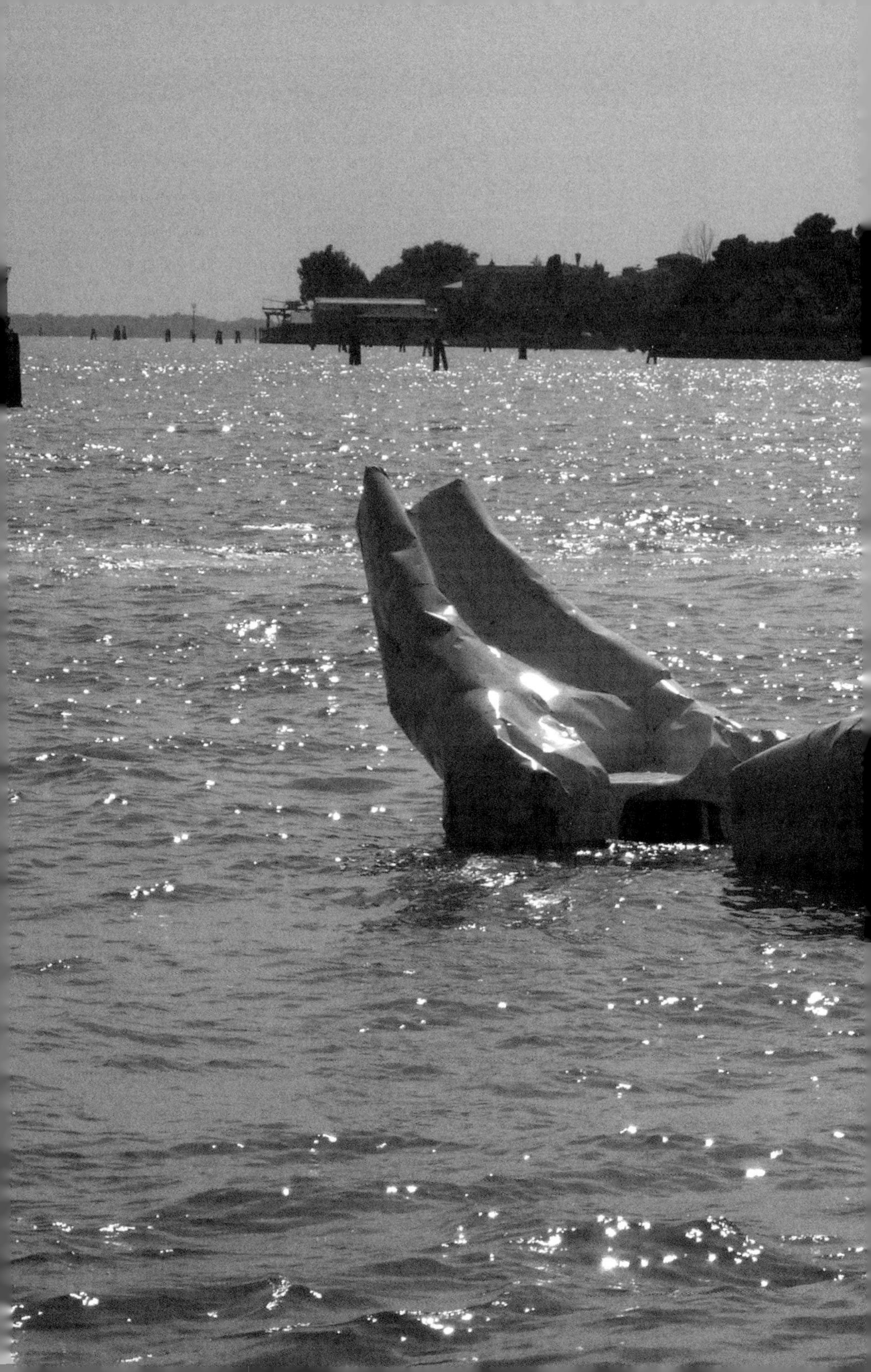

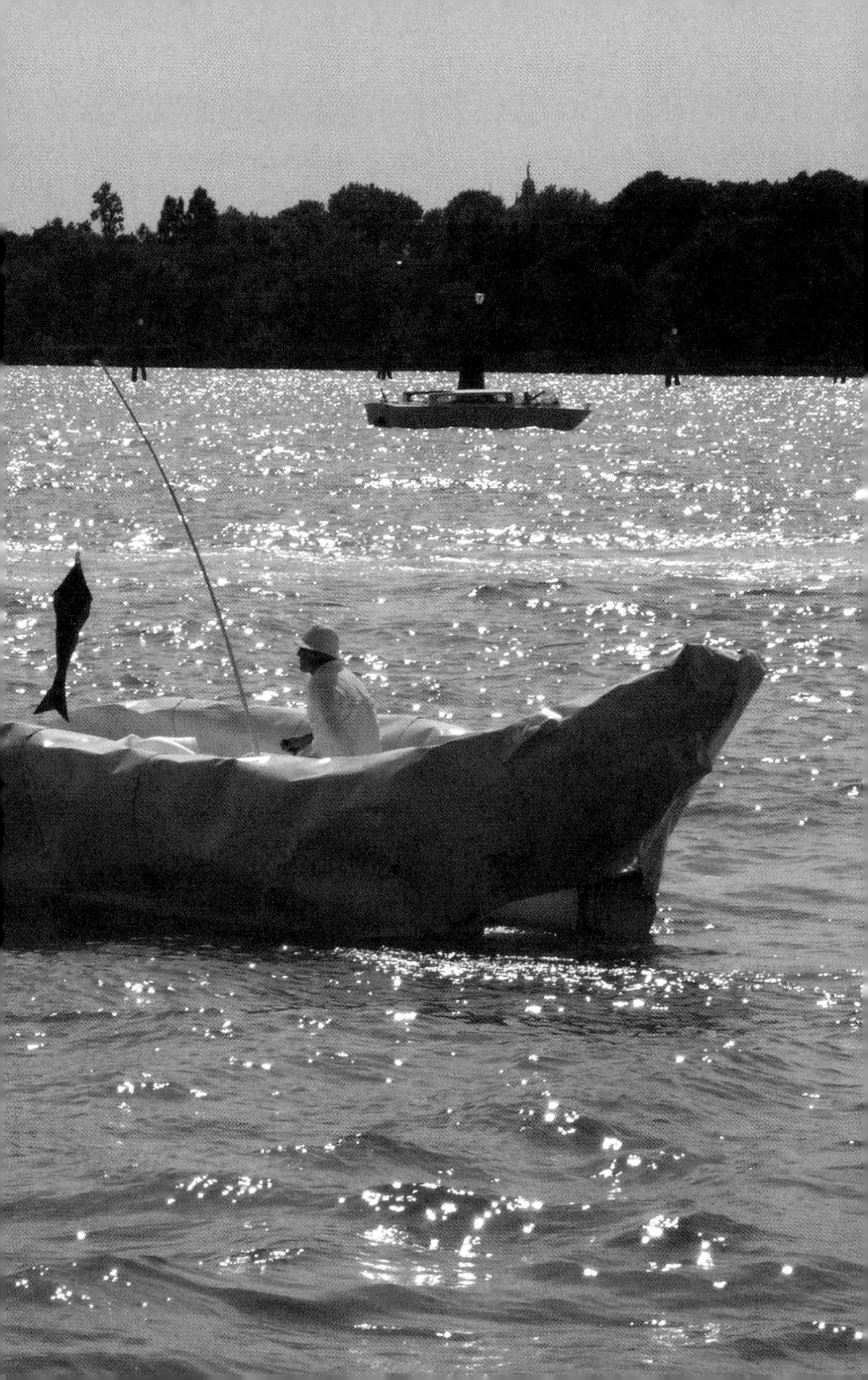

June 4th

I have to admit it: when I viewed the Venice Biennial on June 4th, none of the exhibits stirred me to wonder or reflect. It was definitely a hurried overview. Some reporters and critics might be able to give florid descriptions of things they came across that day, but it would be hard for me. I put my energy into noting how the exhibits were packaged, the system for directing crowd flow, the bookstore layout, and the lighting. Of course there were exhibition halls I did not get to. In fact, to view so many artworks in such a short span of time can dull one's receptivity. Walking out of the exhibition area to the seaside, I gazed at San Servolo in the sunlight. It was not all that far away. On the ocean surface in front of me I noticed a boat made of strange materials, with a dried fish hanging from the boat's mast. There was also a man on the boat, sitting as if he had nothing to look forward to. I felt that I should understand this as one of the expo's artworks, for each viewer to interpret as he saw fit. As for me, even under strong sunlight I felt a slight chill while looking at it. In fact, not many people paid attention to this piece. It was floating in the water at a considerable distance from the exhibition area. But what did it mean to have a symbolic dried fish hanging in midair? As for that "fisherman" wearing white clothes and white hat, I wondered what he was feeling as he sat there hour after hour. I understood the scene according to the most ordinary logic: nothing comes of solitary expectation. This fish was nothing but a symbol and the man's hope was probably pie in the sky. This piece made a deep impression on me, simply because I would

6月4日

我得坦率地承认，6月4日参观的威尼斯双年展中的任何一个展览，都没有激起我的好奇心与思考，的确，走马观花而已。我难以像有些记者甚至批评家那样，对任何一个对象都可以绘声绘色地去描述。我将精力更多地用在双年展览展览的包装，指示系统的设计，书店布置，灯光布置。当然，有些馆我没有去。事实上，在短短的时间里观看如此多的艺术品，在精神与反应上是会迟钝的。走出展区，我在海边上眺望阳光下的 San Servolo，真的很近。我注意到，眼前不远的水面上，有一只用特殊材料做的船，船上一只干鱼被挂在鱼杆上，有一个人坐在船上，似乎没有什么特别的期待。我觉得我应该把这个理解为一件正在参加展览的艺术品。每个观众都可以去解读这件艺术品的含义。至于我，望过去，即便是在强烈的阳光下，也多少感受到一丝凄凉。事实上，没有太多的人去关注这件作品，它在海上，与这个展览区域有明显的距离。可是，一只具有象征意义的干鱼被挂在空中究竟意味着什么呢？那身穿白色衣服，头戴白色帽子的"钓鱼人"长时间地坐在那里会有什么样的感受与内心呢？我还是用最通俗的逻辑来理解这样的情景：孤独的期待是没有结果的，鱼仅仅是一个象征，至于希望，总是画饼充饥。这件作品给我印象多少深一些，仅仅是因为我想我难以做到像那个"钓鱼人"那样孤独地长时间坐在那里，而几乎难以期待有什么奇迹的可能性，我的确没有这样的耐心。这件作品没有什么新的观念，却有一丝悲凉的气息。

这天，张晓刚邀请了几个人在中餐馆"海城"共进晚餐，以为可以在很小的范围内好好的聊天，然而，当我们到了海城饭馆，发现，还是很多中国艺术家和朋友在这里，事实上，大家都非常想念中餐。

find it hard to sit in solitude as that fisherman did, with hardly any expectation that a miracle was possible. I definitely would not have the patience. This piece had no new concept, yet there was a sorrowful air about it.

That day Zhang Xiaogang hosted a few people for dinner at a Chinese restaurant called Ocean City. We thought we could have a good talk, just among the few of us, but when we went to Ocean City, we found that many Chinese artists and friends were already there. In fact, all of us missed Chinese food considerably.

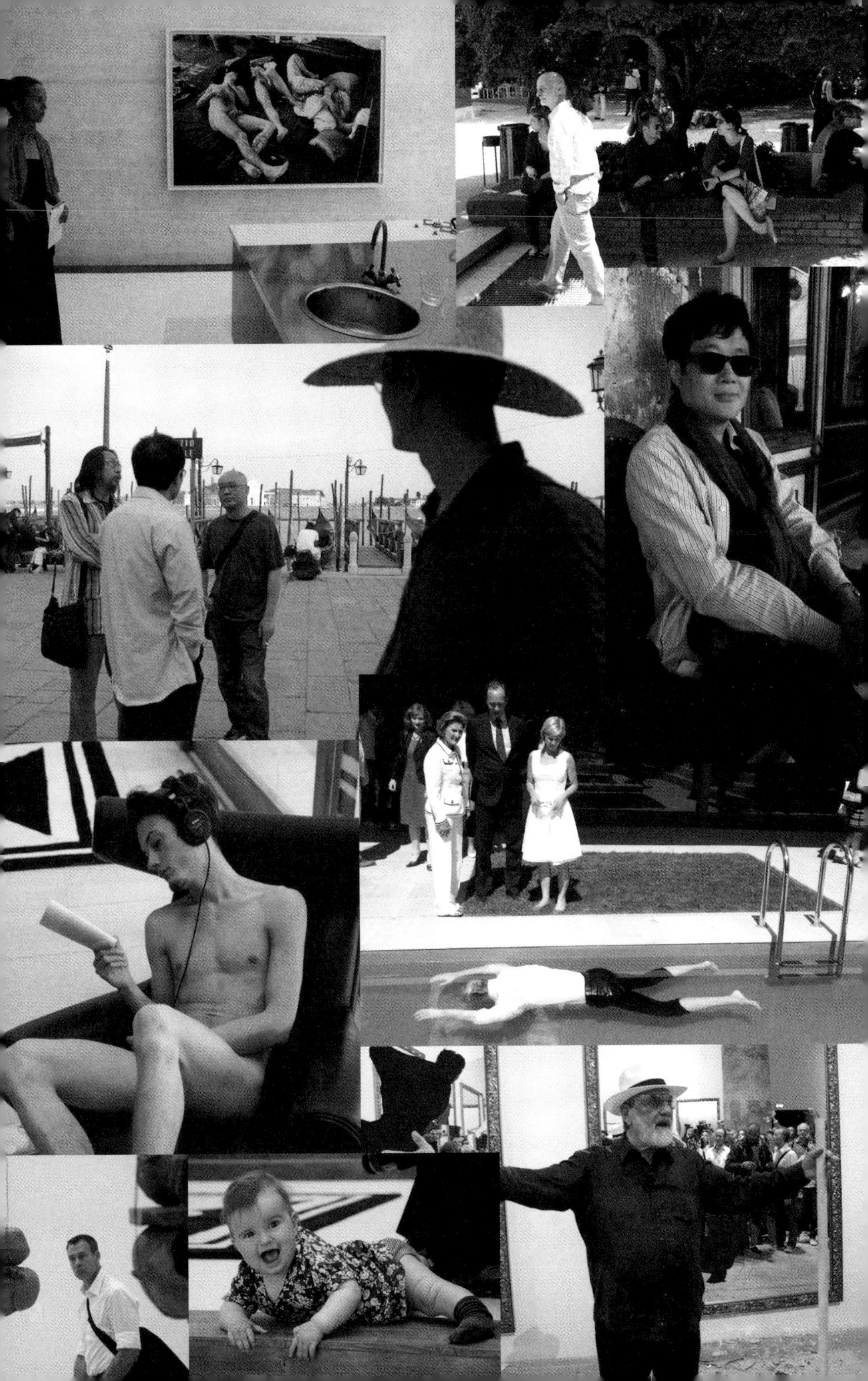

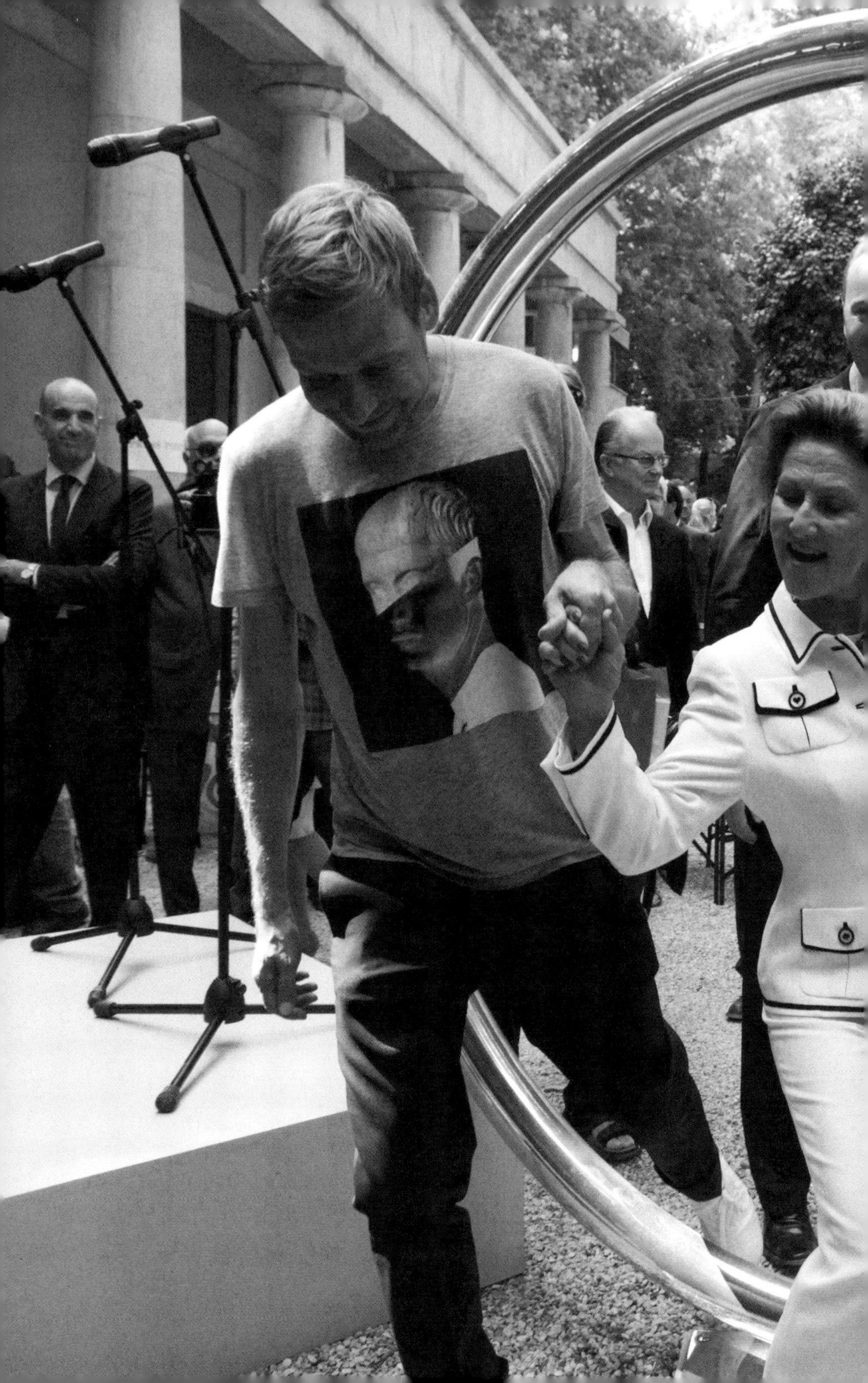

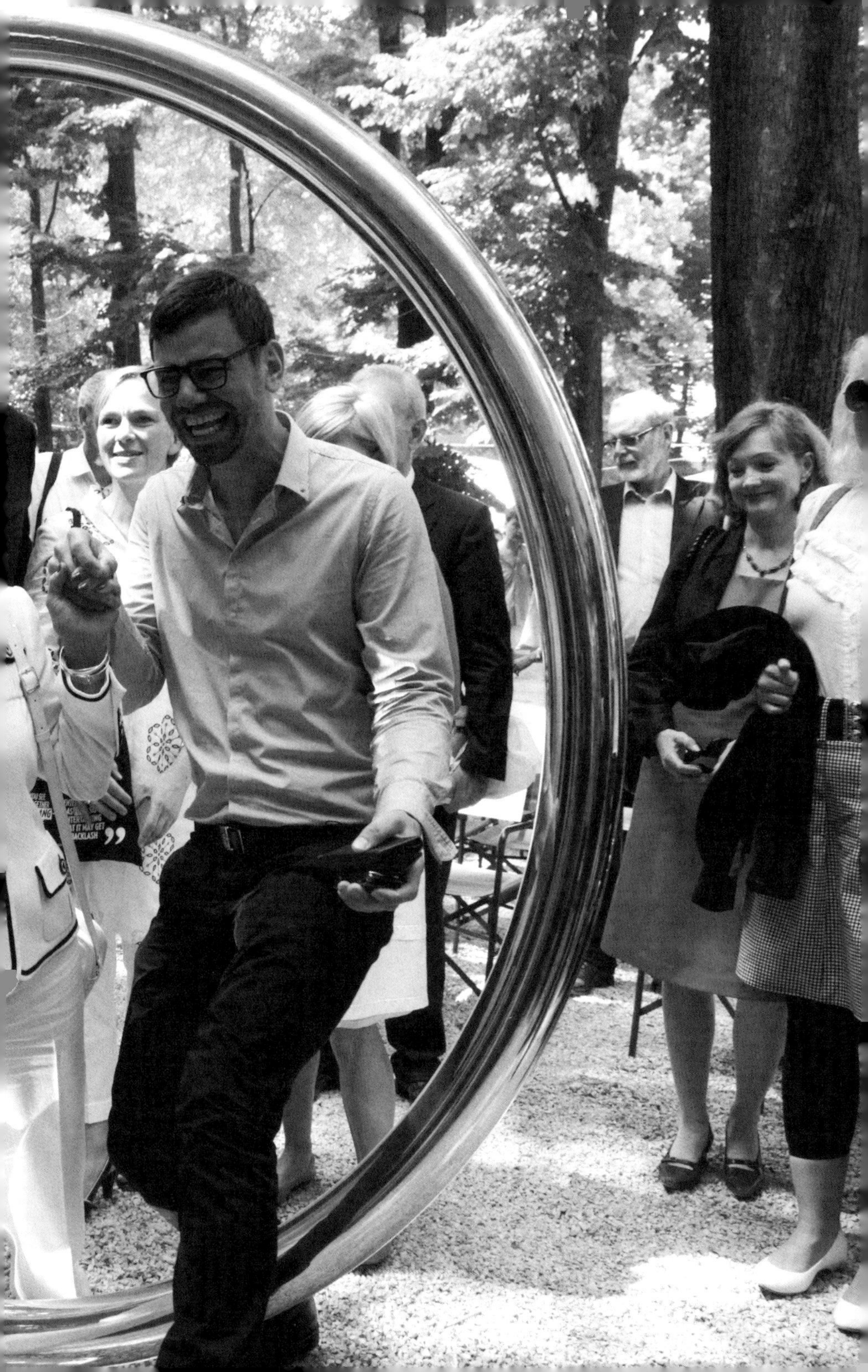

June 5th

At dusk on June 5th, Italian time, we arrived at Amalfi. This somewhat Spanish-looking town has a long history. Founded in 842, Amalfi was Italy's first republic. We took a boat along the Amalfi coastline to Posetano. In the twentieth century this place was visited by Picasso and the French poet Cocteau; one can understand why modernist figures in literature and art were fond of it. In fact, Amalfi was a favored haunt of upper-crust society and celebrities in the 1950s and 60s. The reasons are simple: history, architecture, local folkways, and plenty of scenery to revel in.

During our stay in Amalfi the topic of conversation was still Chinese contemporary art. Perhaps due to current issues—the economic crisis, weak markets, and the proliferation of violent polemics associated with art on Internet forums over the previous two years—everyone seemed to feel that the end of an era had come. Worst of all, before Chinese contemporary art could be discussed or studied in a serious, ongoing, fruitful manner, it was overwhelmed by rampant invective on the web. What, after all, would really be a suitable topic for discussion of today's art? What new perspectives should artists adopt toward our shared world and their own inner worlds? Leng Lin, Xiaogang, and I sat on the patio of the Hotel Miramalfi discussing these issues. I first knew of Leng Lin's name in 1993, when I learned from *Jiangsu Journal of Painting* that Leng Lin had curated the "It's Me" exhibition. Soon afterward I responded to Leng Lin's ideas in the pages of that journal. I do not remember what I wrote, but Ling Lin's reputation and ideas influenced me. A few years later

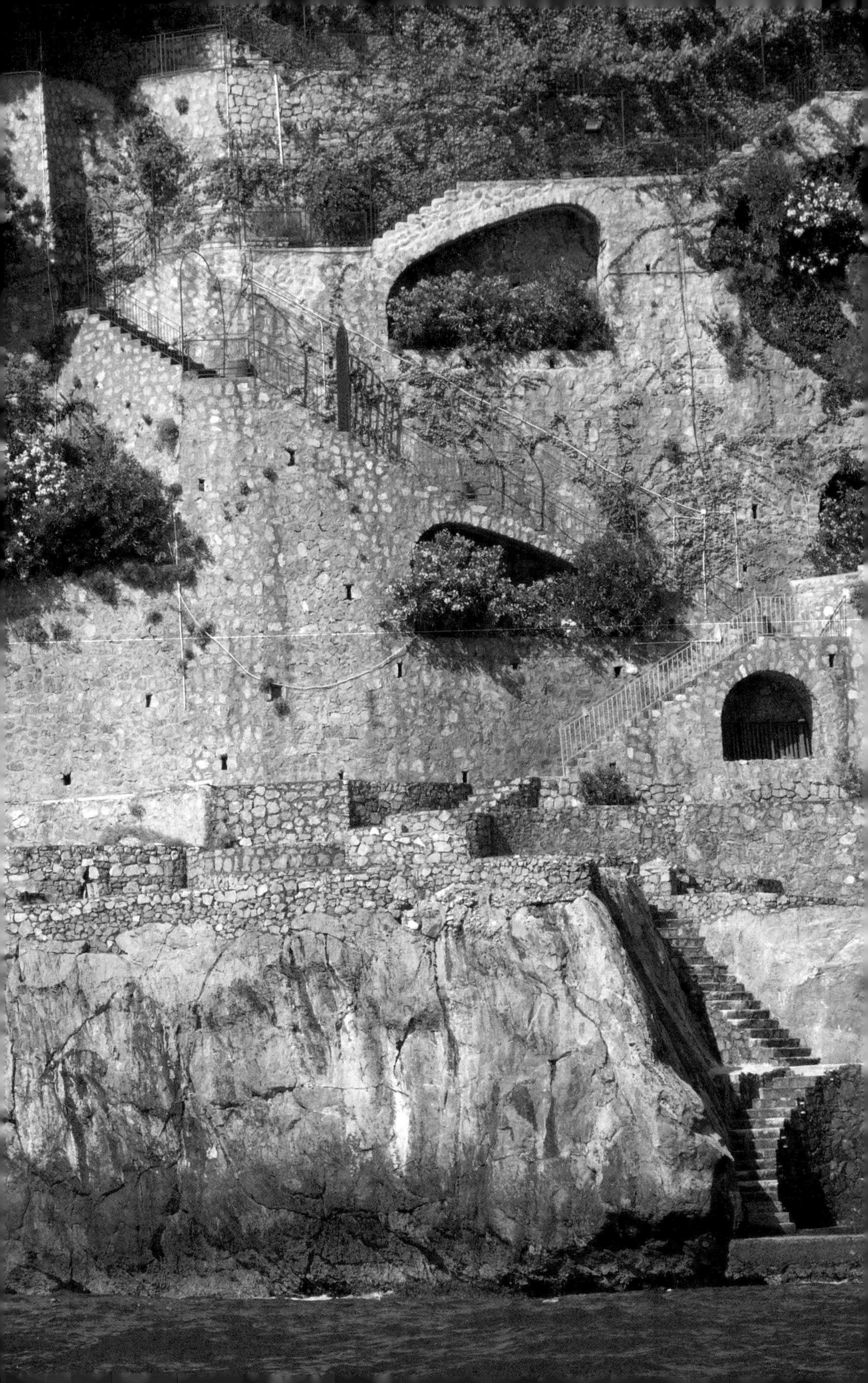

6月5日

意大利6月5日的黄昏，我们到达 Amalfi。这座看上去让人联想到西班牙的小城镇有很古老的历史。Amalfi 是意大利最早的共和国，建于840年。有一天，我们延着 Amalfi 海岸，乘着小船到了 Positano，上个世纪，毕卡索 (Picasso)、法国诗人科克托(Cocteau) 到过这里，能够想象，这里曾经是现代主义文学艺术家喜欢的地方。事实上，Amalfi 海岸在20世纪50、60年代是所谓上流社会与时尚明星经常光顾的地方，原因非常简单：历史、建筑、地方人文以及领略不尽的风景。

在 Amalfi 的几天里，我们仍然讨论中国的当代艺术。也许是在一个特殊的时间：经济危机、市场严重疲软、之前两年关于当代艺术的争论以及语言暴力的四处蔓延，似乎让大家感受到，一个时期真的结束了。尤其是，中国的当代艺术还没有被严肃、持久并富于成果的讨论和研究的情况下，就被网络中泛滥的滥骂给覆盖了。的确，什么是我们今天艺术的真正话题？艺术家应该有什么样的新的视角来观看这个世界抑或观看自己的内心世界？冷林、晓刚、我，我们在H. MirAmalfi 酒店的露天阳台上讨论这些问题。我知道冷林这个名字是1993年，那年我从《江苏画刊》上得知冷林策划了一个展览"是我"，很快，我在《江苏画刊》上回应了冷林的观点。我记不住我说了些什么，但是，冷林的名字和他的观点对我有了影响。几年后，他策划了第一个当代艺术专场拍卖（1996年），成绩如何并不重要，关键是，当代艺术就是在这样的努力下渐渐有了新的发展平台。那天晚上冷林说，现在是需要新的话题和艺术观的时候了。我们经历过了太多的关于东方西方、传统与现代的讨论，经历了很多来来回回的无休止的讨论，可是，在中国获得了全球影响力，中国艺术家和批评家对全球的信息有了自由、轻松的了解的背景下，在经历了三十年

he organized China's first auction dedicated to contemporary art (1996). The outcome is not important: the crucial thing was that by virtue of such efforts, contemporary art found a new platform for development. That evening Leng Lin said that nowadays we need new topics and views on art. We have been through too many discussions about East and West, about tradition and modernity. We have been through interminable back-and-forth discussions. But China has achieved global influence. In a setting that allows artists and critics to absorb global information freely and readily, now that we have been through thirty years of unconfined experimentation, how is Chinese art to carry on? In truth we are facing a crucial pivotal period. In some ways this is like our situation in 1990–91. A historical period of inertia was forcibly interrupted by a major incident. What is the angle or topic whereby we can begin anew?

Amalfi was as beautiful as could be! On our last evening there we walked into an art seller's shop that appeared to have a long history. Nearly everything about the place appealed to me; of course I was most impressed by the artworks and by the exotic Italian taste and style they embodied. In this remote coastal town we could feel for ourselves the esteem in which these cultivated people held their tradition. Those finely crafted artworks and souvenirs were laid out so nicely that we could see how much these people cherished their history and culture. My attention was caught by a depiction of Amalfi in oil. It was not a piece of roadside merchandise in the usual sense. I learned from the owner that this painting had been done by a German painter early in the twentieth century, and that it was priced at a hefty 30,000 euros. It portrayed a portico on a mountain where two old men were conversing, perhaps on a philosophical subject. The creases in their clothes were handled with assurance, and intervening air lent blueness to a distant mountain range. There was a late afternoon slant to the sunlight. The technique was undeniably far beyond the ordinary. I was aware that it was painted in an era when modernism was creating a great stir in Europe. Yet this

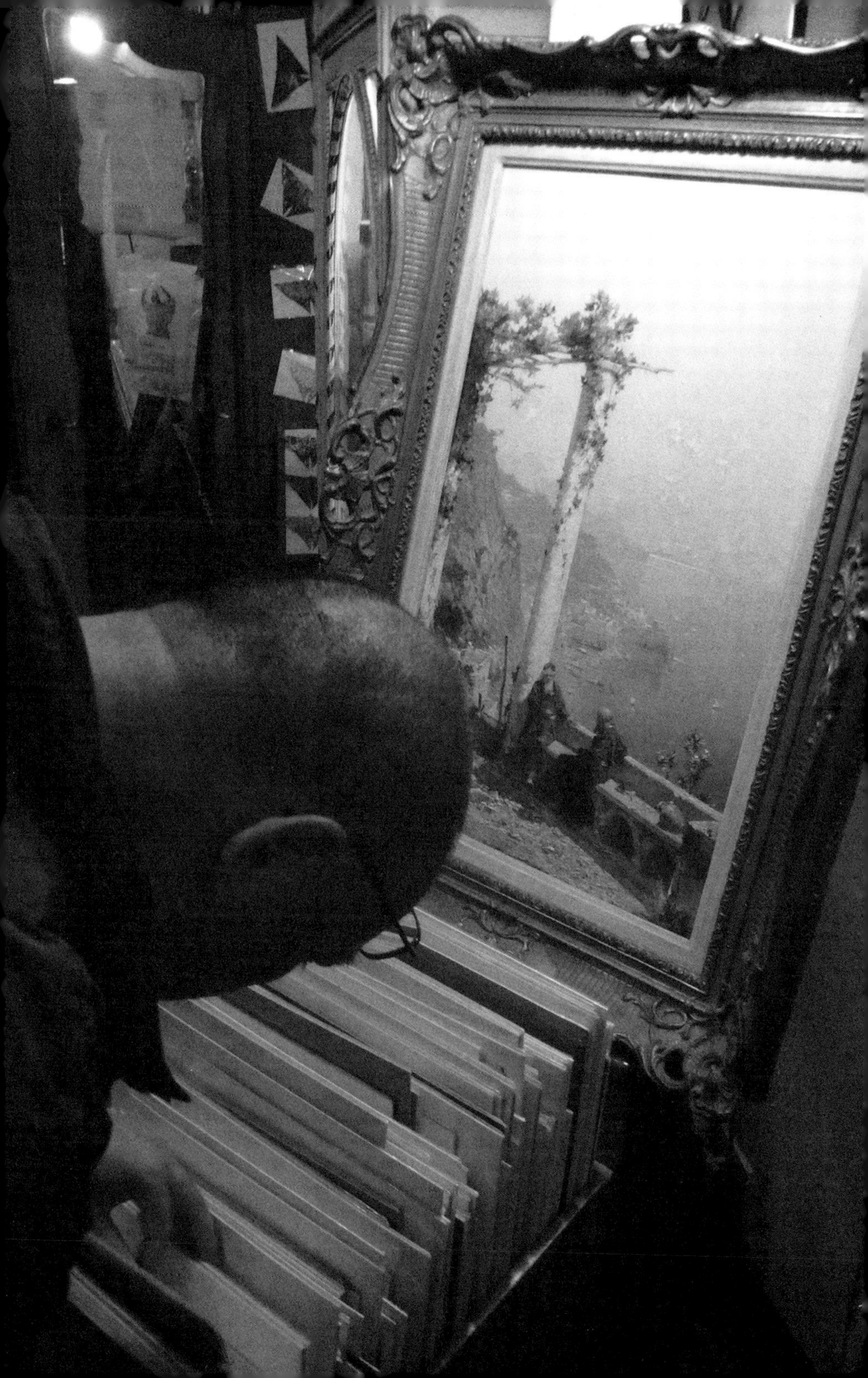

painter, who might have been a professor in an academy, visited Amalfi and was obviously struck by its natural setting and history. What this painter felt inwardly had to have been genuine. To be sure, we can see similar works in many galleries and antique shops. Yet I feel such experience is worthy of the tribute paid to it. To persons engaged in living, we need not invariably apply the criterion of "historicity." To a large degree, with respect to people in the flesh, life itself is the greatest thing of all. At times like this, we can appreciate the value of Kant's maxim. What is more, experiencing life is nothing other than experiencing history. Our traversal of history will always be our spirit's means of growth.

的开放性实验的今天，中国的当代艺术究竟该如果进行下去？其实，我们面临一个重要的转折时期，这多多少少有点像1990、1991年的情况，惯性的历史被一个重大事件给强行中断，我们该从什么角度、话题重新开始？

Amalfi　实在是太美了。最后一天的晚上，我们走进了一个似乎很古老的艺术商店，里面几乎所有的东西都让我喜欢。当然，最给我深刻印象的不是这里的物品的异国趣味、风格与它们的物理呈现，而是在如此偏僻的小镇，我们能够体会和感受到这里的人们对传统的有教养的尊重。那些经过精心制作的艺术品和旅游产品是如此地考究与安排，我们在其中看到、感受到、理解到这里的人们对历史与文化的爱惜与保留。我注意到了一幅描绘Amalfi的油画，我觉得那不是一般意义的旅游商品。一向店主打听，得知，这是一幅由二十世纪初的德国画家画的 Amalfi，价格为三万多欧元，当然很贵。在山上的回廊，两个在讨论也许是属于哲学话题的老人，衣服的褶皱被处理得非常肯定，远处的山脉充满空气，阳光似乎开始走向黄昏，技术无疑是高超的。我当然知道，制作这幅的画的时间正是欧洲现代主义甚嚣尘上的时期，可是，一个可能是学院里的教授到了 Amalfi，显然容易被这里的自然和历史所打动，这位画家的内心和感受，应该是真实的。的确，我们在大量的商店与古玩店里能够看到类似的作品，这样的经历我觉得也非常值得缅怀。对于生活中的人来说，我们不必处处都去使用"历史的"标准，很大程度上讲，对于一个肉身的人来说，生活本身是最伟大的。这个时候，我们也能够感受到康德的那句名言的意思，何况，生活的体验也就是历史的体验，我们的精神永远是在历史的游历中成长的。

June 9th

On June 9th our group left Amalfi for Basel. Only then did I feel that my work had been concluded.

July 27, 2009

6月9日

6月9日的上午，我们一行离开 Amalfi 前往巴塞尔。这时，在我的感觉中，我的工作才真的结束了。

2009年7月27日星期一

List of the photographs / 照片说明

p. 65
Lü Peng and Umberto Vattani, San Servolo, 2009.
2009年5月. 吕澎和翁贝托·瓦塔尼，圣塞弗罗

p. 73
Xiao Quan borrows a boat captain's hat.
船上的肖全（戴帽子的那个）

p. 90
[upper right] Xiao Quan and Lü Peng on the main island, 1 June 2009.
[上右] 2009年6月1日，肖全和吕澎在本岛上

p. 91
[left center] Zhu Zhu and Lü Peng on the main island, 1 June 2009.
[左中] 2009年6月1日，朱朱和吕澎在本岛上
[center] Zhang Xiaogang, 1 June, 2009.
[中] 2009年6月1日，张晓刚刚刚到达
[lower left] Lü Peng and Monica Dematté, 3 June 2009
[下左] 2009年6月3日，吕澎和莫妮卡

p. 92
Zhang Xiaogang and Umberto Vattani at the opening, 2 June 2009.
2009年6月2日，展览开幕式上张晓刚和翁贝托·瓦塔尼

p. 93
Achille Bonito Oliva and the artists at the opening, 2 June 2009.
2009年6月2日，展览开幕式上奥利瓦和众艺术家

p. 94
The entrance to the exhibition hall, 2 June 2009.
2009年6月2日，展场入口处

p. 96
Lü Peng and Achille Bonito Oliva at the opening, 2 June 2009.
2009年6月2日，展览开幕式上吕澎和奥利瓦

p. 97
Achille Bonito Oliva speaks at the opening, 2 June 2009.
2009年6月2日，奥利瓦在展览开幕式上发言
Lü Peng and Achille Bonito Oliva dance at the opening party, 2 June 2009.
2009年6月2日，吕澎和奥利瓦在展览开幕式派对上跳舞
Achille Bonito Oliva dances at the opening party, 2 June 2009.
2009年6月2日，奥利瓦在展览开幕式派对上跳舞
Achille Bonito Oliva dances at the opening party, 2 June 2009.
2009年6月2日，奥利瓦在展览开幕式派对上跳舞

p. 99
Opening celebrations, 2 June 2009.

2009年6月2日，展览开幕式派对

p. 101
Opening celebrations, 2 June 2009.
2009年6月2日，展览开幕式派对
Gao Shiming and Qiu Zhijie at the opening party, 2 June 2009.
2009年6月2日，高士明和邱志杰在展览开幕式派对上
Opening celebrations, 2 June 2009.
2009年6月2日，展览开幕式派对

pp. 104–105
Lu Peng, Zhang Xiaogang, Zhou Chunya and Wang Guangyi, main island,
3 June 2009.
2009年6月3日，本岛的一家意大利餐馆前面：吕澎，张晓刚，周春芽
和王广义

p. 107
Lu Peng and Zhang Peili, main island, 3 June 2009
2009年6月3日，本岛的意大利餐馆内，吕澎和张培力

p. 109
Zhou Chunya, Zhou's wife, Huang Zhuan, Chang Chang and Zhang Peili on
the main island, 3 June 2009.
2009年6月3日，周春芽及其妻子，黄专，苌苌和张培力在本岛
Zhang Xiaogang and Xiaoquan on the main island, 3 June 2009.
2009年6月3日，张晓刚和肖全在本岛
Yue Minjun holding flowers behind Kong Liwen, main island, 3 June 2009.
2009年6月3日，岳敏君捧着一束花在孔立雯身后拍照

p. 110
Cheng Xidong, Wang Guanyi, Zhang Xiaogang and others at a restaurant on
the main island, 3 June 2009.
2009年6月3日，在本岛的一家意大利餐馆内，程昕东，王广义，张晓
刚等人

pp. 112–113
Installation outside the official exhibition, artist unknown, Venice Biennale,
4 June 2009.
2009年6月4日，第53届威尼斯双年展外围装置作品，艺术家不详。

p. 117
[upper right] Uli Sigg, 53rd Venice Biennial, June 2009.
[上右] 2009年6月，乌里·希克在第53届威尼斯双年展现场
[left center] Wang Guangyi, Lü Peng, Zhang Xiaogang, main island, June 2009.
[左中] 2009年6月，王广义，吕澎，张晓刚在本岛
[right center] Lü Peng, main island, June 2009.
[右中] 2009年6月，吕澎，本岛上
[lower right] Michelangelo Pistoletto, 3 June 2009.

[下右] 米开朗基罗·皮斯特莱托，2009年6月3日

p. 121
Amalfi, 5 June 2009.
2009年6月5日，阿玛尔菲

p. 122
Amalfi, 6 June 2009.
2009年6月6日，阿玛尔菲

p. 125
Zhang Xiaogang in an art boutique, Amalfi, 6 June 2009.
2009年6月6日，张晓刚在阿玛尔菲的一家艺术品商店中

pp. 128–129
The coast of Amalfi, 7 June 2009.
2009年6月7日，阿玛尔菲海岸

p. 136
Xiao Quan, San Servolo, 27 May 2009.
2009年5月27日，肖全站在窗前，圣塞弗罗

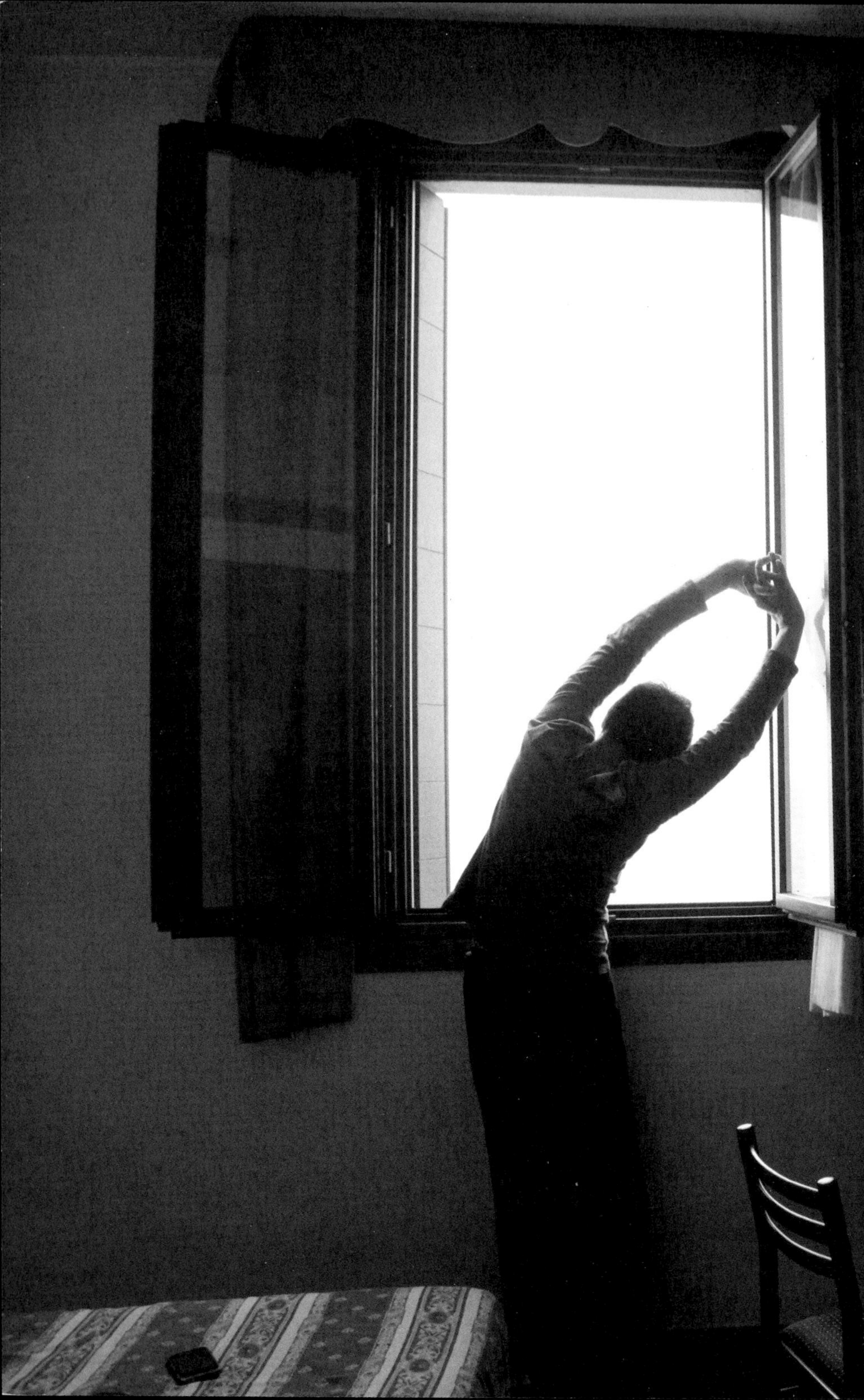

About the Author

Lü Peng is Director of Institutions of CHINART and Associate Professor in the Department of Art History and Theory at the China Academy of Art in Hangzhou, Zhejiang province. Born in 1956 in Chongqing, Sichuan province, Professor Lü graduated from the Political Education Department of Sichuan Normal University in 1982 and was awarded a PhD in critical theory from the China Art Academy in 2004. Lü Peng was chief editor of the journal *Theatre and Film* from 1982-85, and also served as vice-secretary of the Sichuan Dramatists Society from 1986-91. He subsequently held the position of executive editor at the magazine *Art and Market*, and in 1992 he served as artistic director of the Guangzhou Biennale (officially titled the First Guangzhou Biennial Art Fair). His most recent curatorial achievements include "A Gift to Marco Polo" (Venice Biennale, 2009), which showcased eight of China's most prominent contemporary artists, and "Reshaping History" (Beijing, 2010), a massive exposition presenting more than 2,000 works by nearly 200 of the most innovative Chinese artists of the first decade of the twenty-first century.

Lü Peng's extensive publications include: *Modern European Aesthetics of Painting,* (Lingnan Fine Arts Press, 1989); *Modern Painting: New Imagery Language,* (Shandong Literature and Art Press, 1987); *Art-Revelation of Man,* (Lingnan Fine Arts Press, 1990); (with Yi Dan) *Twentieth-Century Art Culture* (Hunan Fine Arts Press, 1990); *Critique of Modern Art and Culture,* (Sichuan Fine Arts Press, 1992); (with Yi Dan) *History of China Modern*

Art: 1979-1989, (Hunan Fine Arts Press, 1992); *The Operation of Art* (Chengdu Publishing House, 1994); *History of China Modern Art: 1990-1999* (Hunan Fine Arts Press, 2000); *Pure Views–Remote from Streams and Mountain: Chinese Landscape Painting in the 10th-13th Centuries* (Chinese People's University Press, 2004); *A History of Art in Twentieth-Century China* (Peking University Press, 2006); *Artists in Art History* (Hunan Fine Arts Press, 2008); *A History of Art in Twentieth-Century China* (Revised Edition, Peking University Press, 2008); *China Contemporary Art in the Historical Process and Market Trends* (Peking University Press, 2010); *A History of Art in Twentieth-Century China* (English Edition, Charta, Italy, 2010).

Lü Peng is also a translator into Chinese of Western texts on art. Among his major published translations are: Herschel B. Chipp, *Selected Letters of Paul Cezanne* (Sichuan Fine Arts Press, 1986; 2nd edition: Guangxi Normal University Press, 2003; 3rd edition: Chinese People's University Publishing House, 2004); W. Kandinsky, *The Spirit in Art*, (Sichuan Fine Arts Press, 1986); Kenneth Clark, *Landscape into Art*, (Sichuan Fine Arts Press, 1988); and various critical writings on Paul Cezanne, Vincent Van Gogh, and Paul Gauguin.

吕澎

1956年出生于四川重庆。1977—1982年在四川师范学院政治教育系读书；1982—1985年任《戏剧与电影》杂志社编辑；1986—1991年任四川戏剧家协会副秘书长；1990年—1993年任《艺术·市场》杂志执行主编；1992年为"广州双年展"艺术主持；2009年策划威尼斯双年展特别机构邀请展"给马可波罗的礼物"，2010年策划在北京举办的"改造历史"展览，2004年，中国美术学院博士研究生毕业，获博士学位，现为中国美术学院艺术人文学院副教授。

主要著作有：《欧洲现代绘画美学》（岭南美术出版社1989年版）、《现代绘画：新的形象语言》（山东文艺出版社1987年版，1999年再版）、《艺术——人的启示录》（岭南美术出版社1990年版）、《20世纪艺术文化》[与易丹合作]（湖南美术出版社1990年版）、《现代艺术与文化批判》（四川美术出版社1992年版）、《中国现代艺术史：1979—1989》[与易丹合著]（湖南美术出版社1992年版）、《艺术操作》（成都出版社1994年版）、《中国当代艺术史：1990—1999》（湖南美术出版社2000年版）、《溪山清远——两宋时期山水画的历史与趣味转型》（中国人民大学出版社2004年版），《20世纪中国艺术史》（北京大学出版社2006年版），《艺术史中的艺术家》（湖南美术出版社2008年版），《20世纪中国艺术史》（增订本）（北京大学出版社2008年版），《中国当代艺术的历史进程与市场化趋势》（北京大学出版社2010年版），《20世纪中国艺术史》（英文版）（意大利charta出版社2010年版）。

主要翻译著作：《塞尚、凡·高、高更书信选》（四川美术出版社1986年版、广西师范大学出版社2003年再版、中国人民大学出版社2004年再版）、《论艺术的精神》W. Kandinsky's The

Spirit in Art,（康定斯基）四川美术出版社1986年版、《风景进
入艺术》K. Clark's Landscape into Art,（肯尼斯·克拉克）四
川美术出版社1988年版等。

Editor / 主编 / Zhao Na

Design / 设计 / Daniela Meda

Editorial Coordination / 编辑协务 / Filomena Moscatelli

Copyediting / 校对 / Charles Gute

Translation / 翻译 / Denis Mair

Copywriting and Press Office / 文案及媒体发布 / Silvia Palombi

US Editorial Director / 美国编辑部主任 / Francesca Sorace

Promotion and Web / 推广 / Monica D'Emidio

Distribution / 发行 / Anna Visaggi

Administration / 行政管理 / Grazia De Giosa

Warehouse and Outlet / 仓储和运输 / Roberto Curiale

Cover / 封面
Xiao Quan, San Servolo, 27 May 2009, photo by Zhao Na.
2009年5月27日，肖全站在窗前，赵娜拍摄

Photo Credits / 图片来源 / Xiao Quan, Lu Peng

We apologize if, due to reasons wholly beyond our control, some of the photo
sources have not been listed.
因为某些不可控制因素，部分图片来源未一一列出，请读者原谅。

No part of this publication may be reproduced, stored in a retrieval system
or transmitted in any form or by any means without the prior permission in
writing of copyright holders and of the publisher.
未经版权所有人及出版方书面授权，任何机构和个人不得对本书任何部分进行
复制、公开展示或转换为其他形式。

Edizioni Charta srl
Milano
via della Moscova, 27 - 20121
Tel. +39-026598098/026598200
Fax +39-026598577
e-mail: charta@chartaartbooks.it

Charta Books Ltd.
New York City
Tel. +1-313-406-8468
e-mail: international@chartaartbooks.it

www.chartaartbooks.it

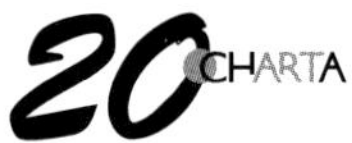

To find out more about Charta,
and to learn about our most recent
publications, visit

www.chartaartbooks.it

Printed in April 2011
by Bianca & Volta, Truccazzano (MI)
for Edizioni Charta